THE
WORLD'S LEADING EXPERTS REVEAL HOW TO GET

MORE

OUT OF BUSINESS AND LIFE WITH

BETTER

RESULTS.

Published by CelebrityPress®, Orlando, FL
A division of The Celebrity Branding Agency®

Celebrity Branding® is a registered trademark
Printed in the United States of America.

ISBN: 978-0-9857143-9-0
LCCN: 2012953681

This publication is designed to provide accurate and authoritative information with regard to the subject matter covered. It is sold with the understanding that the publisher is not engaged in rendering legal, accounting, or other professional advice. If legal advice or other expert assistance is required, the services of a competent professional should be sought. The opinions expressed by the authors in this book are not endorsed by CelebrityPress® and are the sole responsibility of the author rendering the opinion.

Most CelebrityPress® titles are available at special quantity discounts for bulk purchases for sales promotions, premiums, fundraising, and educational use. Special versions or book excerpts can also be created to fit specific needs.

For more information, please write:
CelebrityPress®
520 N. Orlando Ave, #2
Winter Park, FL 32789
or call 1.877.261.4930

Visit us online at: www.CelebrityPressPublishing.com

THE
WORLD'S LEADING EXPERTS REVEAL HOW TO GET

MORE

OUT OF BUSINESS AND LIFE WITH

BETTER

RESULTS.

CONTENTS

CHAPTER 1

THE KEYS TO THE KINGDOM:
HOW TO AUTOMATICALLY MANIFEST YOUR PERFECT CUSTOMER THAT PAYS YOU OVER AND OVER AGAIN AND HOW TO FIND YOUR AUTHENTIC VOICE AND THE COURAGE TO PRESENT AND SPEAK ON CAMERA AND STAGE

BY MIKE KOENIGS

How would you like to attract seemingly "perfect" customers who are affluent, love working with you, buy all your products and services, give you great referrals and keep coming back over and over again?

Several years ago, we sold $9.1 million in products in one week during a product promotion. Six months later, we sold $7.1 million in a single week; $3.1 million was sold in a single day on a live Internet video broadcast. We've repeated this pattern seven more times since then.

Would you like to know how I did it?

At a training event my company was hosting, I met a young guy who was what I considered to be our "ideal customer" because he implemented and made $5,000 in a few hours after implementing one of our software systems to start a new business. His name is "Fireman" Mike Lemoine.

Since then, Fireman Mike has become one of our star customers. *And, we've attracted more like him.*

13

After just a couple of years, Mike's on track to have a seven-figure year income! And using the system I'm about to share with you, we attracted thousands of new customers – and dozens of them with spectacular results.

Many of these customers are closing in on earning over seven-figures using our tools, training and resources. They've built businesses, coaching, and speaking platforms. Most of them built six-figure businesses just a few months after they started working with us.

Less than one year later, I was holding a live event, and I realized we had only about 15 percent women in our audience. I was appalled because I know that the fastest way to create a peaceful, fast-growing, conscious economy and planet is to empower women entrepreneurs. On stage that day, I declared (not having any idea how I'd do it) that we would have 35 percent women in the room at our next event.

Less than a year later, I not only accomplished that, but over 50% of the people in our high-end $25,000 mastermind program are women!

How is this possible?

The following system and exercise I'm going to share with you right now are the "Keys to the Kingdom" – the most powerful marketing strategy I've ever learned or taught. It's the secret to my marketing success and instrumental is having eight consecutive multi-million dollar product promotions in a row in less than three years.

I'm going to get a little philosophical with you now, maybe even a bit spiritual. But I'm going to transform you into an incredible marketer with a 3-minute exercise. And if you're already a good marketer, I'm going to show you how to attract, influence, and deeply connect with your ideal customer.

And if you're terrified of being on camera or on stage and can't imagine yourself writing a book, then prepare yourself for a complete personal transformation.

Have you ever been afraid to fully share your authentic self publicly? Most people are.

However, it's the most powerful way to create a deep connection... Your authenticity resonates with people, and that's what hooks them. That's what makes them want more of anything you offer.

RESONATE

Verb:
Produce or be filled with a deep, full, reverberating sound.
Evoke or suggest images, memories, and emotions.

This is a spiritually based principle, and it's as old as time. But, the truth is, I know this works because I've helped thousands of people unlock their deepest fears about being able to speak or present on video or stage in minutes. I've seen their transformation from putting on a performance to coming from their core... and this switch makes all the difference. The secret is to connect from a place in you that's real, authentic, and raw. Coming from this place will attract your perfect customer to you almost as if it were magic.

Note: Your BS meter may be going off right now. I promise—you will be agreeing with me soon. This works.

If you look back 10,000 years ago or so, early religions and mystical traditions were passed on orally. There were no printing presses and no easy-distribution methods. All information was passed on through stories. Young people were taught by memorizing stories.

Here's how it works. The human brain organizes facts as stories very efficiently. That's why stories about characters and people are easy to remember.

Look at the power of Christianity. The story of Jesus has radically affected billions of people for thousands of years. How? Jesus' disciples and followers had great content (like the son of God resurrecting from the dead). They told stories about the power of forgiveness, love, and transformation that resonated with an audience.

Those stories still resonate deeply with billions of people today!

Fast-forward about 20 centuries. Many consider Steve Jobs to have been the greatest CEO storyteller in the world. It's no accident that Apple became the most valuable company in the world—largely because Steve was able to captivate hundreds of millions of people with stories of what's possible with Apple's products. Steve's stories created massive demand for iPods, iPhones, iPads, and every one of Apple's latest gadgets. Part of Steve's legacy is that Apple will most likely be the first trillion-dollar company in the world! That's the TRUE power of story!

Thanks to Steve and other technological wizards, you don't have to tell your story to one person at a time; you have the power to share your story with the entire connected planet simply by pressing a button. As I said before, you can communicate with nearly the entire human race through a mobile phone, tablet, desktop, or laptop computer.

Think about it. You have more reach now than any person who ever lived less than a century ago!

You can literally record a short video on your mobile smartphone, press a button, publish that video on YouTube in minutes and the entire connected planet with some form of Internet access can watch you *for free*! But that isn't enough to get real attention, develop a real relationship and make money. Something is missing.

Let me show you how to connect with authenticity, to resonate with an audience, and to magically attract your perfect customer into your business or your life. This will also make it profoundly easy to write books and create profitable products. And, as a bonus—this exercise will help make you comfortable on camera, or on stage too.

Sound impossible? Well, let's see...

THE BEST CUSTOMER EVER

This exercise is called, "The Best Customer Ever." I want you to describe the best customer or client you've ever had.

At: www.AuthorExpertMarketingMachines.com, there's a free step-by-step video that guides you through this process in case you're an "immersive learner" like me. Just "opt-in" and you'll get the printable, downloadable "cheat sheet" companion to the video and this chapter.

Who is someone who paid you for your products or services? Think of someone you loved working with. This is a person who took your advice, used your product or service, and got results. They happily paid you (and they keep coming back to you for more). They refer more customers to you, and they give you great testimonials. They're enthusiastic, warm, and happy. Best of all, if you had ten, 100 or 10,000 duplicates of this customer forever, your job would be easy and joyful.

All you have to do is attract more people who are like your ideal customer and you're set.

Write down a description of your ideal customer in as much detail as possible. (Note: If you're just starting out and don't have a business yet, then I want you to *imagine* your perfect customer.)

I'll give you an example of a perfect customer for one of my products. My ideal customer's name is Sue. She's 65 years old, but energetically, she's more like 30. Sue lives in Canada and is a pediatric anesthesiologist. Sue is divorced, has two children, Christopher and Lisa. Sue's biggest fear is that after 35 years of being a doctor, she'll never achieve her dream retirement.

Her greatest dream is to help others live a rich and fulfilling life while traveling around the world... without any financial worries.

That sounds good to me, how about you?

What I like most about Sue is that she is eager, enthusiastic, filled with life, and absolutely passionate about helping other people. The reason I enjoy working with Sue is because she makes a commitment, executes a plan, and gets stuff done.

When Sue started coaching with me, she was afraid she couldn't turn her dream into a book or product. However, after only a single consulting session, Sue got clear on her message, her offer, and her product. She created total clarity on what she really wants.

The next day, Sue sat down in my video studio and told her story with clarity, passion, and vision. In as little as six months, she'll not only be ready to leave her job and have her book and product finished, but she'll be traveling the world, living her ultimate retirement dream while making money teaching others how to do the same.

The greatest wish that I have for Sue is that she'll sell 10,000 copies of her book and be living in dozens of different countries with hundreds or thousands of customers who she can coach in the next year—while making money, feeling purposeful, living fully, and impacting people who resonate with her message and mission.

Done. When you follow this process, you'll attract your ideal customer just like Sue will.

Here's a step-by-step exercise to guide you through this process:

Step 1: Describe the best customer or client you've ever had (and if you're just starting out and don't have a business, then IMAGINE your perfect customer), someone who...

- paid you for your products or services.
- you loved or love working with.
- took your advice, used your product or service.
- got results from your products, advice or service.
- happily paid you and they kept coming back (or will continue to keep coming back).
- refers more customers to you and gives you great testimonials.
- is enthusiastic, warm and happy.
- And best of all, if you only had 10 or 100 or 10,000 of this type of customer forever, your job would be easy and joyful.

Step 2: Now, do the following (this is really easy!):
Hold your phone camera up with your left hand. Press the record button. Smile and put your right hand on your heart. Take a deep breath in, exhale into your heart (breathe nose to heart, imagine the path of your breath following a circle). Smile. Feel gratitude for this moment, in this moment.

Now, think about the best customer you've ever had.

Visualize them standing in front of your camera right now. Smile. Look into the camera and describe her or him. Say hi – say their name. Tell them who their children are. Have a full conversation. Feel them fully, with gratitude and love. Then, look into the camera and *think* about that person while you tell me a story about how you transformed their life or business with your products and services with *passion, enthusiasm, and gratitude.*

I want you to get emotional. This is not a thinking exercise; it's a *feeling* exercise.

So take a moment and record your video.

I can guarantee you, when you do this, you'll never feel or be nervous again – whether you do this on a stage in front of 5, 50 or 50,000 people or on a camera because you're OUT OF YOUR HEAD and IN YOUR HEART.

When you speak from a place of service, love and caring, it's impossible to be nervous. You're not worried about you and what other people think about you. You're focused on someone else.

This is the key. The secret to great marketing.

Speak to the one, don't think, *FEEL.* **RESONATE!**

How did it go?

From this point forward, whenever you make a marketing video, craft an email, create a blog post, or write your book, you're going to speak and write to your perfect customer.

SPEAK TO THE ONE, ATTRACT MANY

It's a little bit counter-intuitive, but if you speak to THE ONE, you will attract many just like them.

You see, if you speak or write to "everyone," you're speaking to no one. You're schizophrenic, and you'll attract crazy, cheap, rotten customers that will suck your life force and all the joy from your job and profession. I call them "psychic vampires" and they'll steal your soul and all the joy from your business, your life and purpose if you let them.

But when you speak to one, more like that person will be attracted to you, almost as if by magic. When you consistently speak directly to your one best customer, you will start attracting more people like him or her.

This is an exercise in manifestation. It is a spiritual act where the physical and the divine become one. Because after all, we *are* all one, right?

YOU CAN DO THIS!

Now look at yourself in the mirror and repeat after me, "I CAN DO THIS!"

You can. Here's proof...

Remember at the beginning of this chapter when I told you I went from just 15% of my customers being women to 35% in less than a year?

Here's how I did it.

During my next product promotion, I read my script to the camera to a new customer I had just met at my event. Her name was Susan (not Sun). She was *real* and heartfelt—someone who represented the kind of woman I wanted to attract as a customer. I knew how old she was, her marital status, her hopes, dreams, her fears and worries. I knew she had a son who was 8 years old and knew what he liked, and knew what she wanted in life—to give back, make a difference and make lots of money to be free. I could imagine her standing in front of me – what she wore and I even remembered what her perfume smelled like. I made her real. I spoke only to her.

When I finished my video, my message was softer, more heartfelt, and more genuine. It was more *real*. My message became attractive to women – because I spoke to one. Only her.

Guess what? Our sales to women nearly doubled from 14 percent to 27 percent. Almost 35 percent of the audience at our next live event was women – entrepreneurs who were very similar to Susan. What's more? This still blows me away. Our high-end mastermind and coaching program is now comprised of more than 50 percent women – and those customers pay us $25,000 per year for this coaching program. I have a dozen people in my high-end 1:1 coaching program that costs $125,000 per year. All of this happened because I practiced this exercise before making my marketing materials.

More recently, we attracted a new wonderful customer named Kristen who was attending that next event. She's a widowed mother of four, spunky as heck, and she earned over $90,000 in three weeks after using one of our systems. What's the best part? She spent only five hours setting up her "Marketing Machines." I don't know about you, but that's the kind of success story I want to share.

This is the power of "The Perfect Customer" exercise. It works for any business, anywhere in the world. I promise you, this is the most significant marketing and training exercise I've ever learned or taught.

But, instead of it taking you 25 years to figure this out on your own like it did me, you can use it right now.

A PROFOUND SECRET

Resonating with your audience is the ultimate secret to really helping people with your message.

You see, people are like crystal wine glasses. When one vibrates, so do the others. The more raw, real, and authentic your message and stories, the deeper the connection will be. You'll magically attract *more* ideal customers. Your message will spread like crazy. This is what will make you go viral.

People appreciate that which makes them feel. There is so much clutter and noise in the world already. But, when you say something real, something of value, something that comes from that place deep inside you that's just being... you, it stands out. People are craving that type of connection in this noisy world. We're tired of being talked at, performed for, and sold to. At the end of the day, we just want authenticity. We just want to know what is honest, solid, and real.

Here's the bottom line—you've got to let your guard down...even if you're scared. You can't hold back. In order to resonate with people, you need to open up and find a grounded space where you are genuinely present and completely candid.

And I believe... no, I *know* it's had a profound shift on the quality of the relationship I have with you right now even if we've never met in person. I also know that if that level of authenticity and rawness offends or pushes you away, then I am not the right person to help you. And I'm OK with that. Great marketing attracts the right people and repels the pests.

This is the deepest and most profound marketing secret I can give you. I have to tell you—eight multi-million-dollar product promotions in a row didn't happen by accident.

I'm not saying this to you to boast. I'm saying this because I've spent 25 years of my life trying to learn the secret to marketing, and it was staring at me in the face the whole time.

Connect with one. More like them will be attracted to you.

So, don't resist the truth. Don't hold back. Be yourself… *your full, true self*. This is the path to your success.

About Mike

Mike Koenigs is a #1 Bestselling Author, "2009 Marketer of the Year", entrepreneur, filmmaker, speaker and holds a patent in "Cross-Channel" Marketing Technology.

Mike is the CEO, "Chief Disruptasaurus" and Founder of Traffic Geyser and Instant Customer. His products simplify marketing for tens of thousands of small businesses, authors, experts, speakers, coaches and consultants worldwide who use these tools to build profitable businesses 2 – 5 times faster than before.

His celebrity and bestselling author clients and friends include Paula Abdul, Tony Robbins, Tim Ferriss, Debbie Ford, Brendon Burchard, John Assaraf from "The Secret", Brian Tracy, Jorge Cruise, Dan Kennedy and Harvey MacKay.

Traffic Geyser distributes video, articles and media to over 100 different social media and social networking platforms with the press of a button that automates marketing — while saving small business owners days or weeks of time and thousands of dollars in promoting their business.

Instant Customer is an automated "cross-channel" marketing platform that captures leads with voice recognition, mobile, online and offline systems — dramatically simplifying and reducing the cost of marketing for small business owners in over 60 different countries.

For over 20 years, Mike has worked with Sony Entertainment, 20th Century Fox, 3M, General Mills, Dominos Pizza, BMW, Ralston and Mazda — creating and implementing innovative high-tech, high-touch marketing campaigns.

Mike's companies have produced eight consecutive online product launches with the largest grossing over $9.1 million dollars and making over $3.1 million dollars in sales during a "direct-to-camera" live webcast.

Mike is the author of the #1 Bestselling book *Author Expert Marketing Machines* and *Instant Customer Revolution,* a book about how to become a highly paid small business-marketing consultant with cutting-edge mobile, video and social media tools.

He executive-produced *Bill's Gun Shop* an independent feature film that was distributed by Warner Brothers and produced a feature documentary, *LifeWithTesla,* about living gas-free with an electric car charged by the sun. That documentary is available free at: www.LifeWithTesla.com.

Originally from Eagle Lake, Minnesota, Mike lives in San Diego, California with his wife and son. He loves the ocean, is an avid boater, fisherman, plays the "didgeridoo" and a variety of other instruments. He strongly dislikes like the smell and taste of canned tuna, egg salad and Brussels sprouts.

Mike can be reached at his personal web site at: www.MikeKoenigs.com.

Connect With Mike
Facebook: www.FaceBook.com/koenigs
Twitter: @MikeKoenigs
Linked In: www.linkedin.com/in/mikekoenigs
YouTube: www.YouTube.com/KoenigsMike
Google Plus: plus.Google.com/+MikeKoenigs

CHAPTER 2

GET OFF THE FINANCIAL ROLLER COASTER
— LEARN HOW TO OVERCOME THE SIX MENTAL CHALLENGES FOR GETTING OUT OF DEBT

BY KEVIN D. HEUPEL, ESQ.

With the recent recession being called the worst economic crisis of our times, many people are struggling with overwhelming debt. Foreclosure rates are high, credit cards are being paid late, and many people feel trapped and wonder if they can ever get out of debt.

Unfortunately, some people get "paralysis through analysis," or feel so overwhelmed by their debt situation that they mentally believe they cannot do anything to solve their financial problems. The good news is that any debt problem can be resolved.

The key to solving a debt problem is to take control and do something about it. However, it's not easy unless you can overcome six mental challenges that keep a person trapped on the financial roller coaster of debt.

THE ROLLER COASTER OF EMOTIONS

Getting into debt is similar amongst people. Most people get into debt for reasons beyond their control. They lose a job, income drops, they have a medical or financial emergency, and they lack three to six months of savings. Without a sufficient reserve, it is common to use credit cards as a way to finance or maintain one's lifestyle. People buy groceries, gas, utilities, and other basic needs with their credit cards while they look for a new job, rebuild their business, recover from illness, or whatever event caused them to use credit as a way to supplement their income.

Using credit can give someone a false sense of security. When you "live" off your credit cards, you don't realize how fast the debt accumulates. If you lose a job that paid you $4,000 per month and used credit cards for six months before you found another position, you would have $24,000 of debt! It shocks people how fast the debt can accumulate when you're using credit with good intentions.

Despite making the minimum monthly payments on credit cards, one's debt either remains the same or increases. It's frustrating to make your monthly payments and realize that it's not doing anything to get rid of it. After a few months or years of making payments that do not decrease the amount of debt, it's very common to panic.

When panic sets in, decision-making is impaired. People will dip into their retirement accounts to pay some of the debt, but not all. Others will sell their personal items to make debt payments. It always amazes me how people will sell their most-beloved items in order to make a credit card payment. It's also sad because they don't feel they have a solution.

Once the assets are sold and gone, people will become distraught and start "robbing Peter to pay Paul." People will transfer debt balances from one credit card to another, ask a parent or friend to cosign a loan, or take a second mortgage to pay off credit card debt. At the distraught stage, a person is taking one bad debt and exchanging it for another.

This cycle can occur over a few months to several years before someone realizes they have too much debt to repay. At this point, people feel like a failure. Most people use debt with the intention to repay their creditors. I rarely meet someone who borrows money with the intent never to repay it. Ninety-nine percent of my clients want to repay their debt. However, the pain associated with financial failure is so strong that most people feel hopeless, stop making their minimum payments, and then have to endure ruthless and nasty collection calls by creditors who reinforce the feelings of failure.

OPTIONS FOR GETTING OFF
THE DEBT ROLLER COASTER

There are typically three options for resolving any debt problem: Credit Counseling, Debt Settlement, and Bankruptcy.

1) Credit Counseling became popular in 2005 when Congress required people who were considering bankruptcy to take a class to learn how to budget. Credit Counseling is where you combine all of your credit cards into one payment at a low interest rate with the goal to repay the debt within five years. It works well if your only debt is credit cards. It does not work if your debt consists of medical bills, judgments against your property or car, personal loans, lines of credit, or other types of debt. Also, the payments tend to be higher than most people's current minimum payments. Thus, if you're struggling to make your minimum payments, then Credit Counseling will be cost-prohibitive.

2) Debt Settlement is a solution that is heavily advertised as the alternative to bankruptcy. Debt Settlement is where you negotiate with your creditors and pay them 20-50% of the outstanding balance. For example, if you have $50,000 of debt, you can realistically expect to settle the debt for $20,000. That's great, but there are some caveats. First, you need to have the $20,000 in the bank. Creditors will not take payments for a settled debt. Second, you have to pay taxes on the $30,000 of debt that you avoided having to repay. Now, instead of having a debt problem, you have a tax problem and having the IRS as a creditor is not fun.

3) The final and typically the best solution is bankruptcy. It surprises many people when I make this statement. Many people think bankruptcy is a crime. Collection companies and debt settlement agencies do a good job of perpetuating the myth that somehow filing bankruptcy is a dishonorable thing to do.

Why is bankruptcy a better debt solution? First, bankruptcy gets rid of most debts such as credit cards, personal loans, lines of credit, overdrafts, payday loans, collection accounts, judgments, unpaid HOA dues, foreclosure and repossession deficiencies, etc. It's easier to state it this way – Bankruptcy eliminates all debts except for child support, alimony/maintenance, restitution, and student loans. Remember, Credit Counseling only works for credit cards.

Another benefit to filing bankruptcy is that you do not pay taxes on the debts you "discharge" (i.e., eliminate). Bankruptcy is tax-free whereas Debt Settlement creates a tax problem.

The next benefit is that you get to rebuild your credit sooner. It typically takes two years to restore your credit after filing bankruptcy. It's very possible to have a credit score in the 700s within two years of filing bankruptcy, qualify to buy a home with a FHA mortgage, obtain credit cards again, and buy a car at a low interest rate. It takes seven years to recover from Credit Counseling and Debt Settlement.

The final and best benefit is that you can keep the things that are important in order to get a fresh financial start. You can keep 100% of your retirement. That way, you're not sacrificing your financial future for a debt problem that exists today. You can also keep a home, car, furniture, personal items and jewelry that are reasonable in value. Bankruptcy allows you to recover from a financial mistake without imploding your life – no other debt solution can do that.

OVERCOMING THE EMOTIONAL CHALLENGES TO GET OUT OF DEBT

Resolving debt problems by filing bankruptcy is easy. However, finding the emotional courage to file can be challenging. Here are six emotional challenges that one needs to overcome in order to decide if bankruptcy is the right solution.

Emotional Challenge #1:

TRUST – Reliance on the integrity, strength, ability, surety, etc., of a person or thing; confidence.

Creditors have an uncanny ability to destroy a person's trust. A bank will give someone an overdraft account, line of credit, car loan, and multiple credit cards based on a "credit score" and the assumption that the person borrowing the money will pay it back. However, once you are late on a payment or struggling to repay debt, the bank will lower your credit limits, raise your interest rates, make negative reports on your credit history, and basically make it even more difficult to repay your debts. Many of my clients say that if the creditor would just work with them, they would repay the debt. But most creditors won't, and as a result, people lose their trust in potential solutions.

Every American has a legal right to get out of debt. Bankruptcy is a federal law first enacted by Congress in 1800 and approved by President John Adams.

The federal bankruptcy laws have their origins from the Bible. Nehemiah 10:31 states: *Every seven years we will let our fields rest, and we will cancel all debts.*

Another reference can be found in Deuteronomy 15:1-2: *At the end of every seventh year you must cancel your debts. This is how it must be done. Creditors must cancel the loans they have made to their fellow Israelites. They must not demand payment from their neighbors or relatives, for the Lord's time of release has arrived.*

Bankruptcy is something we can rely upon to get out of debt. Its origins and purpose are to restore "trust" by giving people the chance to rebuild their financial futures. My bankruptcy clients have confidence that they will get out of debt, rebuild their credit, and keep their important possessions. They "trust" the bankruptcy laws and legal system to help them rebuild their financial lives.

Emotional Challenge #2:

PERCEPTION – The act or faculty of apprehending by means of the senses or of the mind; cognition; understanding.

Overcoming the emotional challenge of perception requires you to face your worst enemy – YOU. If you think bankruptcy is not an option, then you need to change your "perception" of bankruptcy and look at the positive aspects of getting help. You need to realize that many famous and successful people have filed bankruptcy. Walt Disney and Sam Walton both filed bankruptcy. Were their lives a failure because they filed bankruptcy? Heck No! They rightfully perceived bankruptcy as a financial tool that they could use to eliminate their debt and try again. We should be thankful that they filed bankruptcy as Walt Disney brought great entertainment to our country and Sam Walton forced companies to sell their products at affordable prices to all consumers.

Emotional Challenge #3:

COURAGE – The quality of mind or spirit that enables a person to face difficulty, danger, pain, etc., without fear; bravery.

People will avoid bankruptcy because they "fear" the outcome. Many people think they will lose their homes, cars, and retirement if they file bankruptcy. This is simply not true. The only way to overcome the fear of bankruptcy is to have the "courage" to call a bankruptcy attorney and review their financial situation. Most bankruptcy attorneys offer a free consultation. I recommend that you meet with at least three attorneys to make sure you are getting consistent advice. I'll explain later in this chapter about how to find a competent and reliable bankruptcy attorney.

Emotional Challenge #4:

ACCEPTANCE – The act of assenting or believing.

Overcoming this emotional challenge requires you to "accept" the reality of your financial situation. When you have unsecured debt that is more than 20% of your gross income, you will never repay the debt due to compounding interest rates. Even if you are making your minimum monthly payments, you will not pay off the debt because it is too much. You can get out of overwhelming debt by "accepting" that bankruptcy is a reality.

You have to face the facts. Not accepting the reality of your debt problem keeps you stuck and unable to live a productive life. You can't live in the present and plan for the future if your head and finances are stuck in the past.

Life is just as it should be. Make the best out of any situation. You can't change reality by wishing your debt problem had never happened. Accepting the reality of your situation and living fully within your reality facilitates letting go of the past and moving ahead to the future. A future you carve out for yourself is based on what you want, not based on where you used to be.

Emotional Challenge #5:

BELIEF – To have confidence in the truth, the existence, or the reliability of something, although without absolute proof that one is right in doing so.

One of the first steps to financial success is belief in yourself. You have to "believe" that you are doing the right thing for you and your family. Believing in yourself is all about being sure that you are going to do whatever is right for you, even if others are against you.

Your friends and family will have their opinions about bankruptcy, and remember it is just their opinion—not fact and not the truth. Your friends probably know less about bankruptcy than you do, especially if they have never struggled with debt. Some people think that unless everyone agrees with them then they are doing the wrong thing. This thinking is self-destructive. Stop thinking that other people's opinions are important and concentrate on what's best for you.

Emotional Challenge #6:

FEAR – A distressing emotion aroused by impending danger, evil, pain, etc., whether the threat is real or imagined.

One of the greatest fears that someone has when filing bankruptcy is how their friends and family will react. No one wants to feel judged or rejected.

Clients constantly ask me if bankruptcy is a public record. Yes, bankruptcy is a public record and there are some newspapers that will print the names of people who file bankruptcy. However, it is very difficult to know if someone has filed bankruptcy, as it requires you to search for a specific person on a database known as PACER, which typically only attorneys use.

Regardless if your bankruptcy can be found, I recommend that my clients tell their family and friends. You would be surprised at how many of your friends and family are supportive and will help you emotionally as you go through the process. This even applies when your friends and family did not think bankruptcy was a good idea.

There is no reason to live in "fear" of other people's opinions. Nothing others do is because of you. What others say and do is a projection of their own reality, their own dream. When you are immune to the opinions and actions of others, you won't be the victim of needless suffering. The best way to overcome this "fear" is to live an open and honest life with those you love.

EMOTIONAL RELIEF LEADS TO HAPPINESS AGAIN

The good news about bankruptcy is that you do not have to go through the process alone. I always recommend that anyone considering bankruptcy should hire a bankruptcy attorney. Remember, bankruptcy is a federal law that is governed by legal rules and procedures. Lawyers are trained to handle the process to ensure that you get out of debt. When people file bankruptcy without an attorney, typically, the results are worse and could have been avoided with proper planning by a lawyer.

When hiring a bankruptcy attorney, I recommend that you visit with three attorneys and gather as much information as possible. This will help you understand the bankruptcy process and determine if there is a certain "style" of lawyer you like. Not all attorneys are the same and it's important that you hire someone you respect.

Be sure to only select attorneys who specialize in bankruptcy. Bankruptcy is complex and has a long history of case law unique to its practice. You wouldn't hire a dermatologist to perform heart surgery and lawyers are no different than doctors when it comes to specialization.

Hire an attorney that files a large volume of cases – at least 500 per year. Expertise can only be obtained through experience. Some smaller bankruptcy attorneys try to discredit larger firms, but volume is proof of experience. This year, I will have filed more than 4,000 cases in my career, which means it is a rare day that a financial situation is too complicated for me to handle.

Finally, ask the attorney if he or she has any money-back guarantees. Once I meet with a client, I can predict with 99% accuracy as to the outcome of his or her bankruptcy. I offer money-back guarantees so that the client knows they can rely on my recommendation that bankruptcy is the best solution. Otherwise, why gamble with your financial future?

The financial roller coaster of debt can be exhausting and mentally challenging. When you step off the financial roller coaster and overcome the six emotional challenges, you can live a brand new life. In the bankruptcy world, we call it a "Fresh Start." Everyone is entitled to recover from their mistakes and unforeseen events that lead to debt. There is no shame by filing bankruptcy. The real shame is not doing anything. If you are struggling financially, then take action today and get help. Life is too short not to be enjoyed!

About Kevin

Kevin D. Heupel, Esq. is a debt relief attorney who has helped thousands of people get out of overwhelming debt. Kevin is the founder of Colorado Bankruptcy Experts and is the largest filer of bankruptcy cases within Colorado.

Immediately after law school, Mr. Heupel served as an Assistant Attorney General for the State of Colorado. Mr. Heupel prosecuted a variety of cases where he honed his litigation and negotiation skills and earned the public trust. As a result, Mr. Heupel is well-versed in solving complex debt problems.

Prior to practicing law, Mr. Heupel was a corporate accountant. His legal and accounting experience enables him to understand his client's issues in order to find appropriate and practical solutions.

No one wants to file bankruptcy, but it helps to have an experienced, knowledgeable attorney and accountant in your corner who cares about you. Kevin Heupel understands the emotional and financial challenges that people face when they have too much debt to repay. To help his clients, Kevin offers a money-back guarantee and the ability to file bankruptcy for $0 down.

People who need a debt solution need to connect with Kevin Heupel – a debt relief expert.

To learn more about Kevin Heupel, the debt relief expert, visit: www.HeupelLaw.com, and to learn more about filing bankruptcy,
visit: www.ColoradoBankruptcyExperts.com.

CHAPTER 3

GET A G.R.I.P. ON YOUR RETIREMENT

BY BRADLEY M. OLSON CPA/PFS

The two things you can do to create a retirement free from financial uncertainty and fear.

In my over 20 years of planning client's retirements, I have found the number one problem for people in retirement is financial uncertainty and fear of 'going broke.' The retiree should have a WORRY-FREE retirement. In this chapter, you will find great information to take action on, information that cannot only provide you with the retirement that you deserve, but the retirement for which you saved your whole life. You deserve a retirement that is one WITHOUT worry, one that has reasonable asset growth, and one that has the capability for GUARAN-TEES and peace of mind.

The retirees that have placed their trust in the stock market system have learned the hard way that that system is set up for failure for retirees. You only have to look at the last eleven years to figure that out. With the historic declines in the stock market over that time frame, it's no wonder that many a retiree's dreams of a worry-free retirement were crushed. Nobody can predict when the next market crash will come, but you can avoid them, and I can show you how with my G.R.I.P. system for retirement.

My G.R.I.P. system is the only system that promotes and provides GUARANTEES and SAFETY. The institutions and strategies used in my G.R.I.P. system have been around for over a century and have proven time and again when the market corrects itself, their products are unaffected. It's the G.R.I.P. system that has been providing this protection and will always be the system of choice for the retiree. It provides certainty, guarantees, and financial security.

PUT YOUR RETIREMENT MONEY ON CRUISE CONTROL

Many people who have retirement money are understandably aware of portfolio risk (or volatility), or at least they think they are. Now, what we are really talking about here is downward volatility, aren't we? (No one minds or complains about UPWARD volatility.) Anyway, what do most people do when they are trying to reduce the volatility in their retirement money? What has been the message from the stock market advisor system that people have heard over the years? "Diversify between stock and bonds," right? Well aside from the inherent, serious flaws in this advice, what are they actually trying to do? Aren't they trying to take a portion of their money and take it out of the market so it isn't subject to large decreases?

First a little background. The world of investments can be divided up into two basic worlds, (a) the world of Protection and (b) the world of Potential. First, the world of Protection, or safety. The world of Protection is made up of three basic types of investments, bank certificates of deposit, US government treasury bonds, and fixed annuities from legal reserve insurance companies. What do all of these investments have in common? First, the principal is guaranteed, second, the interest is guaranteed, and third, the term (or length of time) is known, and generally there are penalties for early withdrawal. The second world is the world of Potential (or growth and risk). Investments in this area include stocks, bonds, mutual funds, options, commodities, real estate investment trusts, variable annuities, etc. What do these types of investments have in common? First, the principal is NOT guaranteed, the interest (or earnings) is NOT guaranteed, the Term is open ended, and generally you need time for these to be effective, but the amount of time can vary greatly. There have been downturns in the market that took 20 years or more to recover. Does someone in retirement want to wait that long for their money to recover from significant losses? Probably not.

So traditionally, a person had to choose between investments from the world of safety, where they would get a very low return, but their money would be safe. Or they could try to get a higher rate of return with an investment from the world of Potential, but their money would potentially be subject to significant, and sometimes catastrophic, market losses. In the past few years, a third investment world has been developed, the world of the "Hybrid" or "cruise control" investments. This world consists of only two alternatives, the Equity Linked CD which is issued by a bank, and the Hybrid, or Fixed Index Annuity, issued by a legal reserve insurance company. These investments start with the safety qualities from the world of Protection (Principal and term is guaranteed). The difference is that rather than having a fixed interest rate, the interest or earnings on the contract are linked to a market index from the world of Potential. What this allows the investment to do is have the good qualities from the world of Protection and yet have the opportunity to earn a rate of return much higher than has been possible before. These Hybrid investments are NOT invested directly in the stock market.

The FIA puts the retirement money on cruise control. It automatically keeps the money protected when times are bad in the market, and allows the retirement money to earn a higher rate of return than traditional "safe" investments when the market is good. Just like the cruise control function in a car, the FIA keeps your retirement money moving ahead safely. This is a very effective tool for investing retirement money for most retirees. The problem is that most people don't know about them, or have listened to the stock market advisor media propaganda of bashing these types of investments. Now, I'm not saying that this type of product is appropriate for everyone, but it is GREAT for the retiree. And really, is there any one single financial vehicle that is best for everyone at all times? I don't think so, because at different times in your financial life, there are different priorities, and as you move through the different times your investment philosophy has to move with you.

GUARANTEE YOUR RETIREMENT INCOME

When it comes to your income in retirement, that income should be guaranteed to come to you no matter what. It should NOT matter what the markets do, or do not do. Your income should come to you regardless, and it should come to you for the rest of your life. Guaranteeing your income is now your number one priority.

This is probably the most heart-breaking mistake a retired American can make. Imagine that you are cruising through retirement, happy as can be. You do what you want to do, when you want to do it. You don't have a care in the world. But then, the markets collapse, like they did twice in the 2000's. And suddenly, you see your retirement portfolio evaporating in front of your very eyes. Your portfolio values are dropping because of the market AND to compound the problem, you are pulling money out at the same time. This is a "double whammy" and your retirement assets are diminishing faster than you ever imagined. This is actually called "**reverse dollar cost averaging**." It is devastating to a retirement portfolio and unfortunately, I see it happening all the time.

What happened? You made the classic mistake of not guaranteeing your income in retirement!

When it comes to your income in retirement, that income should be guaranteed to come *no matter what*. It shouldn't matter what the markets do, or do not do. Your income should come to you regardless, and it should be there for you for life.

During the 90's, you could read any publication or watch any financial news network and read or hear about the mutual fund or investment of the year that posted double-digit returns. The American retiree became mesmerized by the investment returns on their statements and lost track of what the higher purpose of those statements represented.

And, then the "stock market bubble" burst.

For many retirees this was the beginning of a long-forgotten lesson about risk on Wall Street. You take risk with your "play" money, NOT with your retirement money. In 2007 and 2008 the financial system finally collapsed with the largest market meltdown since the Depression. Portfolios vanished. Even the regulatory agencies, who were supposed to have the job of protecting investors, failed to do their job. It was a complete failure from the top down. People who counted on their retirement portfolio for security were now devastated. What they worked their whole life for was, in some cases, completely gone.

Think about how you would have felt if your retirement income was guaranteed and what happened to the markets had absolutely no effect on your income. You still get to travel, go out to dinners, visit your grandchildren, help your kids out. Basically continue doing what you want to do when you want to do it, to be able to keep your retirement dreams intact. Do you think you could sleep at night under those circumstances? I think so.

How do you do that? You simply use the G.R.I.P. system to set up your retirement portfolio. The G.R.I.P. system simply allocates enough of your portfolio in the Hybrid guaranteed products to deliver you the level of income that you want to have in your retirement. It's fine to use risk assets for the extras in life, but not to generate your income. Your retirement income needs to come from these guaranteed products.

There is much confusion out there about how to create income when interest rates are so low. American retirees are trying to figure out what to do with their stock market retirement portfolios. Politicians are talking about higher taxes in the future and entitlements ruining our financial system. So, what should you be thinking about? Not "investing" but protection and guarantees. You need to think like a lottery winner. If you have enough income guaranteed to be coming in no matter what, do you really care if taxes go up a little? Do you care about stock market investment strategies? Do you really care about getting every penny from market gains? Do you care about how much money you have, as long as you have all the income you need? The answer is probably "NO." Ask yourself these questions, "Do I want to be a retirement investor or do I want to be a retirement winner?" The G.R.I.P. system guarantees that the American retiree becomes a "retirement winner!"

If you are dealing with stock market investments, you will NOT be able to guarantee your income and principal. Stock paying dividends, mutual funds, bond funds, etc. will NOT be able to guarantee your income. They all have risk.

As crazy as this may sound, there are millions of American retirees who have no idea how they will create the income that they will need to sustain their lives. The stock market advisor system has not shown them how to do it. Their system is all about investing the money and all of the different choices, formulas and schemes to invest. It's not about guaranteeing the goal of having a secure and guaranteed retirement. Retired Americans are just now finding out that their strategies that they used to grow their retirement savings are not working for them. Just look back at what happened the last 11 years. Many are finding themselves running out of money when they cannot go back to work, and are now having to rely on children and grandchildren for the basic needs to survive. That is a pathetic, and totally preventable, tragedy. Please understand this!

The G.R.I.P. system can guarantee your income 100%. No questions asked. Look at your current retirement accounts and think about what I just said. What part of your retirement investments has the guarantees that you need?

I cannot state this goal more emphatically: YOU MUST GUARANTEE YOUR PRINCIPAL AND INCOME!! I have given you a lot of information to think about and use to your advantage. There is only one system that works for the retiree, that is my G.R.I.P. System for retirement planning. It is the only system that can provide you with the guarantees and protection that you need in your retirement. If you use my G.R.I.P. system then you can live a worry-free retirement. Let me help you.

About Brad

Bradley M. Olson CPA/PFS has over 20 years of professional experience in planning and securing retirees financial futures and is the founder of Olson Wealth Advisory, a premier retirement planning firm in Cincinnati, OH.

Brad has degrees in Accounting and Economics, is a licensed CPA and has earned the prestigious AICPA PFS (Personal Financial Specialist) designation. He holds over a dozen other licenses and designations and continues to improve his professional knowledge base by attending several advanced planning industry meetings held throughout the year. He is a highly sought after speaker, and has attended and spoken at many national conferences.

Brad is also a proud husband and father of three happy, healthy, active children.

CHAPTER 4

TRAINING YOUNG ATHLETES

BY JIM PICKFORD

Having been born and raised on the Canadian Prairies, maybe my first athletic experience isn't that unique. There are many memories lost to me, but I remember this moment as if it were yesterday. I would have been four or five years old, Mom and Dad bundled me up and took me onto a slough, one mile away as the crow flies, for my first skating lesson.

My parents were in their big winter boots and I was in my snowsuit and skates. Come to think of it, I actually do not recall if I had a helmet on, that may have been the first of my many concussions. I remember not wanting to let go, resistant to stand on my own which, without a doubt, sent my Father into a rage. This led to the next part of the lesson. One… two…three, "launch across the ice and figure it out" training method." Oh it was magical, like I was born with skates, I just took off skating! Not even close! It was a corpse pose across the wind-polished ice, my nose acting as my brake pad and crying my eyes out.

Fast-forward thirty-six years. I am a High Performance – 1 Coach and IYCA Level 3 Youth Fitness Specialist, combined with over twenty years of playing and twenty plus years of Coaching Hockey from Initiation to MM AAA – not to mention having my own five children involved in minor hockey ranging from Initiation to MM AAA. I have gathered a boatload of knowledge that will assist you and your young athletes towards achieving their true potential.

I wish that I could say that I did not learn the hard way, but I would be lying. I have made too many mistakes to remember, both as a Coach and a Parent. My wish with this chapter is to provide an opportunity for you to learn from my life's experiences and continued pursuit of knowledge, while hopefully avoiding my pitfalls. You have the chance to save time by doing it the right way.

To best accomplish this task, I have comprised a Top Three 'Must Do' List to help your young athlete reach their true athletic potential:

1. DREAM BIG

There are numerous books written on the importance of goal setting. Using the subconscious mind as a weapon aimed directly at attaining any goal. Without dialing in the subconscious mind, the chances of attaining greatness will be severely limited. Depending on the mental age of the athlete and the loftiness of their goal these things will dictate how goal setting will look. The purpose of goal setting is to get the subconscious mind working on attaining the task as well as mapping out a step-by-step action plan. By using the acronym SMART (specific, measurable, attainable, realistic, and timely), you will ensure success.

Each young athlete may be stimulated in different ways, depending on the style of learner they are and their age. The two most important things for parents to remember in supporting their child's dream are as follows:

(a.) Ensure the dream is not their own unfulfilled dream passed down to their child. If that is the case the motivation will not be pure intrinsic motivation but extrinsic which will not provide enough fuel to attain a dream goal over the long haul.

(b.) Be your athlete's biggest supporter. During times of great success and when they fail forward, regardless of what anyone says, does, or thinks; your number one priority is that your athlete must know you love them unconditionally, regardless of sport performance. Enjoy watching your child compete in their sport regardless of wins/losses, great plays/mistakes.

The young athlete should utilize one of these options to help reinforce their dream goal:

Motivational Poster (4 – 18 years of age)

- You will need scissors, glue, tape, colored paper, white paper, stickers, crayons, magazines, a photo of your athlete, and any other craft supplies.
- Have your young athlete (or parent) cut out quotes, pictures of their favorite athlete, team, their team, animals, etc.
- Place their photo on the center of the white paper and ask them to write (or the parent can write) "My Dream Is…."
- Have the athlete create their visual masterpiece and cut, paste, color, and write about their dream goal or goals in life.
- Let them take charge and you are there only to assist when asked.
- Once this is completed have the poster laminated and hang it in their room, take it to their practices or games, school, or whenever they want.

I have completed this task with athletes that were four years old to sixteen years of age. This powerful visual tool can also be used for short term and long-term goals not just Dream goals. While coaching a peewee team in Drayton Valley we decided to have athletes build a goal-setting poster to prepare them for another provincial championship run. We actually built individual identical championship banners out of poster board and had each athlete write what it would take from them for the team to do its absolute best. Young athletes are brilliant, they know what they want and it is much more powerful when they voice the importance of things like hydration, nutrition, rest and preparation versus the coaching staff doing so. What a great bunch of athletes and parents. I was truly blessed to be part of that group.

Mind Movies

This will entail a personal highlight reel of their athletic accomplishments like footage from practices or games, movie clips, famous quotes, picture of their animal within, family, heroes and whatever else inspires them. This can be a very powerful tool to help continually guide them towards their goals.

The technology is amazing now, and we actually utilize a system called mind- movies, which is an amazing tool to help simplify this process.

I would strongly encourage all coaches and especially parents of young athletes to formulate a goal-setting formula that will work for their young athletes – to keep their motivation high and focused on their goals.

2. BOOST CONFIDENCE

How many of us as adults remember the vehicle rides to and from sporting events? Are the memories positive or negative?

As a young athlete, I was always extremely happy when we would car pool or take a bus, because then I wouldn't have to listen to my Dad verbally destroy me. I know that he was only trying to help, as many loving parents still try to help their kids today.

The youth sporting world has changed a ton since I played on natural ice in Paradise Valley from November to February. Professional athletes are paid very well and appear to live a dream life. When our young child tells us they want to be an athlete, we need to ramp up our game to a new level of crazy. Kids as young as seven are playing one sport year round. This appears advantageous short term, physically however, long term it can have adverse effects both mentally and physically – with burnout and chronic overuse injuries.

In the book *Raising An Athlete*, Jack Perconte, a former major league baseball player would be asked many times, can you make my son a major leaguer. This is his response: "…there are no shortcuts. It all starts with the love of the game, followed by hard work, which produces success. Those three, love, hard work, and success build upon and feed off each other. No one can make a player a major-leaguer; only the player can do that."

Coaches and parents are instrumental in helping the athletes attain all three of the "real performance enhancers."

"The most important natural performance enhancer is love. People who love something will have fun working on it. The best way to develop love for a sport is to have fun playing and there is no better way of spurring a young athlete to want to work on a sport than to make it fun." Jack goes on discussing the importance of creating a practice environment that is fun.

Understand the important role you, as parents, have in this process. Both verbal and non-verbal forms of communication will either build your athlete up or tear them down. You as a parent are given numerous opportunities to instill confidence or self-doubt. Make a conscious effort to build confidence. This will pay huge dividends in all aspects of your young athletes life.

As a former Junior hockey player who definitely lacked confidence, I have dove into that subject to look for why I was the way I was. After reading many books, researching respected sites on the Internet, I came to the conclusion that I created this sense of self-doubt aided by negative coaching, and reinforced during the ride home from the rink.

What can we as parents do to build confidence in our young athletes? The answer is simple, live a block from the rink. (So your Dad doesn't have time to critique your performance.) Even that doesn't work, ask my eldest son Austin. He is fifteen years old and plays hockey at an elite level. We live a block from the rink and he has told me he wants feedback, however, could I please wait twenty-four hours until I give him any feedback.

Seriously now, here is a list of things you can utilize to help grow your child's confidence no matter what the sporting event:

(a.) Always tell them how much you enjoyed watching them compete and play the game. Be sure to find at least five amazing things you noticed them do at their sporting event.

My nephew Dexter, who is four years old, has just finished his first stage of Chemo treatment for a very rare form of Leukemia. He was trying to play tag with my three boys and his brother. At one point Dexter could not even walk up the stairs, and had to pull himself up by the hand rail to get up the last step. Why am I sharing this with you?

Please keep things in perspective. Your child is playing a game they love. You have to try and understand that there is a lot going on in their body. They are not always going to be at 100%. Love them unconditionally and be the one 'for sure' safe place they can come to.

Dexter started out at the dermatologist's office with a rash on his face and the next thing our family is sitting in an office with a Doctor writing on a white board explaining the battle that amazing little man has to fight to survive.

How many of us with kids in violent, dangerous sports actually give thanks and are grateful that our child is safe and sound after competition. This would be Step two.

(b.) Be grateful and thankful for your child being able to walk, talk and take part. Most importantly, tell your child you love them even when they stink at their sport.

(c.) Talk about your child's strengths. You can do this verbally or in writing. Write notes in their school lunch, discussing why you are proud of them, and build that sense of self-worth so they can take pride in themselves. Find quotes that discuss confidence and self-worth and put them on mirrors, blackboards, vehicle windows, etc.

There are great short stories or powerful novels that one can call upon to either read to your young athlete or have them read themselves. I cannot think of a better story than David and Goliath, which is my three little guys favorite bedtime story, depicting the courage and confidence God had given David. (If we lack confidence ask through prayer and it will be given.)

(d.) Create Mental Toughness in your athlete. No matter how hard you try as a parent you will fail forward and make mistakes. Your athlete will be exposed to people who try and take away their positive energy. The athlete needs to develop an impenetrable wall of toughness.

In the book *Hockey Tough*, by Saul Miller, he talks about how to create a mentally tough athlete. Here are a couple of pointers from his book:

1. Stay on the power channel.
   Think of your mind as a TV and you are holding the remote. If you don't like what you are watching, hearing or thinking, change the channel. The puck goes off your skate and into your own net. You skate back to the bench and your coach, who by the way if he does this should not be coaching, tears you a new

one. After the verbal abuse has stopped from your coach, if you want to perform you must learn to 'park, get rid of, and throw away.' Imagine it as breathing. When you breathe out, get rid of negative energy, body language, tone, hurtful words and breathe in positive energy.

2. Create an Animal Within.
   Think of an animal whose traits you admire and are like yours or how you visualize yourself competing.

My son Austin, at the age of nine, watched a wolverine fight off a pack of wolves. The team he played for were called the wolverines. He was a smaller athlete and found a suitable animal within he could relate with. Therefore, when you are switching channels to get back to the power channel, Austin would watch a wolverine fight off a pack of wolves. I am a wolverine; I am tough, fast, strong, and smart – rather than negative self talk like 'I suck,' 'my coach hates me' 'my team hates me for scoring on myself.'

"At the highest levels of sport it is 90% mental and 10% physical."

I remember as a youngster watching Hockey Night In Canada, and seeing players make glaring mistakes that would cost their team. I would think why doesn't he hang his head, bang his stick, swear or something. He would just skate back to the bench like nothing happened. That I know now was a display of *Mental Toughness*.

3. PHYSICAL TRAINING

I was fourteen years old and I attended Jr. A spring camp. At this camp, I was introduced to weight training via a super set. The training was comprised of barbell military press, reverse curls, bicep curls, decline pushups, upright rows and then you completed three sets of ten reps in seven minutes.

I remember one of the guys asking, "what do we do for the legs?" The answer I heard was they get enough training when you skate.

So this is the program I followed for about two years, plus, I added in some bench press, tricep and bicep work. I got strong, dysfunctional and injury prone, and looked like I was riding a chicken – my legs were so scrawny.

I played in pain from 17 – 20 years old. My whole junior career and while I thought I was training to improve my hockey career, I was actually stacking strength on dysfunction – which will always end the same. The body breaks down and pain and injury are the end result. I had no idea what to do. I was told no more hockey, quit lifting weights or I will be in a wheelchair by forty years old.

These were things that I did not want to happen to my son. When Austin was playing spring hockey, he was exposed to leading edge off ice training, or that was what I was told. I remember the sales pitch being Jarome Iginla trains here and come and train like Jarome Iginla. Jarome is an adult NHL hockey player and my son was ten! It bothered me at the time but I really didn't have the solution or any better ideas. I saw a real problem with how young athletes were being trained.

After my exposure to Brain Grasso and the International Youth Conditioning Association (IYCA), I have long since learned why that isn't the ideal situation and what should be done. Their story of Jarome Iginla being cut from Alberta Cup Team (top 2nd year bantam age players in Alberta) to then go on to NHL stardom still rumbles through Alberta arenas. As a parent you should be interested in what Jarome did at fourteen after he was cut, that propelled him to stardom – if that is your child's dream. Compare this to exposing a child to watered-down adult programs for our youth.

PARENTS TOP 3 MUSTS FOR ATHLETES

As a Youth Fitness Specialist (YFS Level 3) I would recommend that you search for a Long Term Athletic Development Model versus a six –week – increase vertical leap by 6" – program.

To ramp up my learning curve, I have studied from the leading strength and conditioning coaches in the world. I cannot recall who said this (whether it was Mike Boyle, Joe Taft, Eric Cressey or Mike Robertson), but it was stated that a quality program should provide the athlete three things in this order:

(1) Never get hurt training

(2) Decrease chance of injury in your sport of choice

(3) Increase performance

As a current IYCA member, I would strongly encourage you as parents to take action, and either educate yourself through the IYCA or expose your young athlete to a quality program that has been field-tested on over 15,000 athletes. Give your child the advantage of being a healthy, strong, functional athlete.

Parents I wish you all the best in supporting your young athlete.

Dream Big, Build Confidence and Train Smart!

About Jim

Jim Pickford has been coaching young athletes for over 2 decades, dating back to 1990 as a hockey and fastball coach to hundreds of aspiring athletes. Jim has been running hockey skill development camps throughout central Alberta for the last 10 years for local minor sports organizations, teams and specialty camps. There are many young athletes that Jim has had the pleasure to coach over the years that have went on to play on Team Brick Alberta, Bantam AAA, Midget AAA, Alberta Cup, AJHL and University hockey. More importantly, many young men are now professionals in the work force with families, leading healthy, happy lives.

Jim played 4 years of junior hockey in the AJHL for the Lloydminster Blazers and appearing in one All-star Game. Now looking back, Jim is the first to admit that improper training technique, leading to numerous preventable injuries, was definitely one of the contributing factors to not achieving his full athletic potential. After coaching for 10 years utilizing outdated approaches to physical and mental training, Jim stumbled across the IYCA. This was a perfect match for what Jim was looking for and ultimately led to the opening of the first International Athletic Revolution in Leduc, Alberta.

Jim and the Athletic Revolution Leduc staff are excited to provide the central Alberta area with a World Class option for young athletes ranging from the ages of 3 to 18 an opportunity to develop their athletic genetic potential in a professional, enjoyable and healthy environment. Fun and Fit for LIFE!

<u>Jim's Training and Certifications include:</u>

<u>(I). International Youth Conditioning Association</u>

Youth Fitness/Conditioning Specialist-Level III

High School Strength and Condition Specialist

Youth Speed and Agility Specialist

Youth Olympic Lifting Instructor Course

Youth Kettle bell Instructor Course

Youth Nutrition Specialist Level I

<u>(II). NCCP</u>

Level II Theory

Level I Olympic Lifting Trained

(III). Hockey Alberta

Initiation Coach Certified

Coach Certified

Development I Certified

Development II Certified

High Performance Trained

Speak-out Certified

Safety Certified

CHAPTER 5

IMPROVE YOUR HEALTH USING KEY COMMUNICATION STRATEGIES

BY VICTORIA GROVE

Hi. My name is Victoria Grove and I appreciate the chance to help you get the most from your doctor visits.

I have learned a great deal about health care over the past three decades. I began in awe watching the doctors and nurses bustling about, stethoscopes around their necks, taking care of the sick, the injured and sometimes doing what seemed impossible. One such instance from one of my hospital experiences continues to haunt me. A beautiful young woman was brought to our ward after she had accidentally caught her hair in an office machine, pulling off her hair, scalp and even an ear. The surgeons worked valiantly for sixteen hours attempting to put her back together. Although the first attempt did not work, other strategies were attempted to help this unfortunate woman.

What I also observed over the years were needless tragic outcomes due to rushed, careless professionals, missing important details but moving ahead with their plan nonetheless. My work was done in many healthcare settings, including hospitals, clinics and physicians' offices. My role typically involved evaluating problems in process and communication, which gave me a comprehensive understanding of what constitutes quality care. Among other reasons, poor patient outcomes can result from medical errors. Many of these are generally well-known by students of health care and have received media coverage.

One area less well-known is the role of communication in medical mistakes. When you are recognized for your knowledge of health care and medical processes, it is not uncommon to be approached by people sharing their feelings and concerns about their own medical care. After listening to numerous stories of pain, frustration and in some cases lost hope, I began to see a common thread emerging from their experiences. While some were attempting to cope with untreated conditions of a chronic nature, such as pain or unidentified clusters of symptoms, most had been to more than one medical professional hoping to find relief from suffering. Regarding pain, it is important to treat it in the early stages. Otherwise, it can turn into chronic pain, which can baffle physicians and last for years.

What these stories suggest is that something has gone awry in communication involving the physician, clinic or hospital employees, and the patient. These patients were clearly distressed and many felt hopeless. It should be made clear that no matter how busy a medical practice or hospital station is, suffering connected with untreated or unidentified disease must be remedied. In fact, some states have laws that address this. Clues as to the source of the patient's problem are often uncovered during a careful discussion between doctor and patient. Information such as when the symptoms began, what else was happening during that time, and how the patient's quality of life was affected, are crucial places to begin. Listening takes time, which is often shortchanged in the medical environment, but the importance of attending to the medical history from the patient's viewpoint cannot be overstated. Some of these problems seem to occur when the patient's disease is not well understood. It is not unusual for a patient to go from doctor to doctor in order to find one who will treat their suffering in the absence of a well-established diagnosis.

Communication is not just talking; it may also be nonverbal. Some patients' nonverbal behavior suggests a negative attitude. This may cause the physician to react in a negative manner, leading to unintended consequences. Some examples of non-verbal communication are posture, facial expressions and failure to establish periodic eye contact. (Obviously, it is not desirable to hold a stare for twenty minutes, no matter how pleasant the look.)

Another story is significant as an illustration of how even minor errors in communication can lead to tragic consequences. A man in his forties was diagnosed with a brain tumor and had surgery to remove it the next day. The symptoms soon returned, necessitating another surgery. The surgeon's nurse erroneously recorded in the patient's chart that he had overused pain medications. This happened because the patient had had a previous surgery on his upper spine that did not go well, and he had been given opiate pain medications for a period of time. The patient's girlfriend took advantage of her access to self-treat her headaches, so when they were needed for the young man's condition, a phone call to the doctor would be necessary. Because the quantity of medications ordered was greater than the nurse expected, she made the assumption that the overuse was the patient's.

After the second brain surgery, the young man did well and was discharged two days later feeling optimistic. Later that day he developed a severe headache with fever, chills and convulsions whenever he tried to lift his head. In the ambulance, he vomited and lost consciousness. At the Emergency Room the doctor who treated him read the nurse's note stating that the young man had been overusing pain meds. That doctor, busy and accepting the note as diagnostic, decided to treat him with Narcan, a medication that reverses the effects of opiate overdose. Shortly after this while being taken to Imaging, the patient experienced a cardiac arrest. He was revived, had a breathing tube inserted into his lungs and was admitted to Intensive Care Unit (ICU). Five days later he was rushed to surgery when his condition rapidly deteriorated. The surgeon discovered significant deadly bacterial meningitis, which had become so advanced during the five-day hospital stay that it had destroyed a section of his skull. Sadly and ironically, the pathology report had just returned showing no new growth of the cancer. What the surgeon had believed to be a return of the cancer leading to the second brain surgery was tissue damage related to the radiation therapy, a condition for which surgery was not helpful.

The doctor who was responsible for the young man's care in the ICU had not been made aware of the complaints that resulted in his E.R. visit. Instead, he was managing the patient for drug overdose and subsequent cardiac arrest. Nothing in the patient's chart indicated otherwise. On day two of the ICU admission, the neurosurgeon visited his patient to give him the good news about the pathology report. Trusting his nurse, the surgeon was also treating his patient's admission as a "drug overdose," although he did note redness and swelling in the patient's neck on the side where the brain surgery had been. Nothing in the management of the case was changed in the subsequent care of the young man. The patient never recovered from this series of mistakes, shortcuts and misunderstandings. Within two months, the patient expired at the age of 47. It is my belief that the original source of the misunderstandings was the nurse who had incautiously noted "overuse of pain medications" on the patient's chart without adequate evidence. This error reverberated through the health care team at a time when the patient could not speak for himself.

Your visit with the doctor may be for something as simple as a hangnail. It could be something much more complicated, requiring more "thinking" time to figure it out. Typically medical providers have twenty-minute appointments. New patients referred by other doctors may be given an hour for a consultation. However, follow-up appointments are typically twenty minutes.

A few of the many healthcare time stealers are: after being put into the exam room, a nursing assistant begins with a series of questions (and weren't many of them answered on that form you filled out in the waiting room)? The assistant leaves you, telling you when the doctor should arrive.

Ah, a knock on the door means the doctor is coming in. This is one of the most important twenty minutes for the patient. The doctor will spend perhaps one or two minutes in the introduction phase. Next, the doctor spends a few minutes looking at your chart, followed by asking why you are there. (If you were counting, you have used about six minutes; 14 minutes left).

As you begin to answer the question, another time thief knocks on YOUR door and speaks to the doctor for 45 seconds, followed by your doctor leaving to deal with something (NOT YOU!).

About five minutes later, the doctor returns. You and the doctor are beginning to feel the busyness of the clinic and the passing of time. "Now, where was I?" The doctor decides the pain you were attempting to describe was probably from food choices. You are given a quick exam, which doesn't identify anything specific. The doctor gives you a brief explanation, hands you a prescription for gas and tells you to return in three or four months if the problem doesn't resolve.

Out the door goes the doctor. In comes the assistant. Out you go.

The doctor was probably relying on prior experiences occurring with other patients; most of the time that probably works. What if your case is something more different or more serious?

NINE WAYS TO IMPROVE YOUR HEALTH – USING SIMPLE COMMUNICATION STRATEGIES

Here are some things you can do to get the most out of your twenty minutes and to make sure you do not become a victim of poor communication. Always prepare for your medical appointment using paper or note cards.

1. Note your reason for the visit and list all the information related to this problem. For example: If you have been having pain, note where it is on your body. If you can draw a body, note on the picture where the pain is. Consider when you first noticed it. There are several words that may help describe pain, such as: dull, sharp, burning, spasm-like, constant, off and on. Pain intensity is usually measured from one (hurts the least) to ten (worst imaginable). Note anything that makes it better or worse: bending over, lying in bed, pressure on it, how it responds to cold or heat or touch.

2. If you have already tried treatments with only minimal improvement, this is important information to provide. Also, if you have seen other providers for your pain, note this as well, including what treatment was done and how effective it was.

3. After you have made all the notes, put them in order of importance, placing the most important first.

4. Politely let your doctor know at the beginning that you intend to be an active partner in your care. This will identify you as a thoughtful patient who not only will be cooperative, but also will be highly motivated to get the best possible treatment.

5. On subsequent visits, continue to bring note cards with a summary of any changes in your condition following the advice you have been given. Be as specific as you can. If you were not helped by the first treatment, this could mean that the doctor needs to consider a different treatment or medication change. It could also mean the doctor needs to reconsider the diagnosis. If so, the sooner the message is received, the more likely you are to get an accurate diagnosis and appropriate treatment.

6. Although doctors are knowledgeable and tend to be caring people, they are also human. For many reasons, mistakes are frequently made in medical settings. When you show your respect for your doctor (or other provider) but also make it clear that you are providing an accurate history and educating yourself about your problem, you will find that your doctor will be a better listener.

7. If you have the feeling that your doctor does not understand what you have tried to explain, schedule an appointment to discuss it. Take all of your notes and be prepared to review the previous visits with this provider, what you were told about your situation and why you believe your treatment is not helping your condition.

8. If the individual has a problem in hearing, comprehension or memory, it is advisable to have a relative or friend attend the appointment with the patient to assist in this process.

9. Don't give up. If your doctor is not helping you, it could be time to find another one. You can contact your insurance company for assistance. The State Board of Medical Review is also a resource for finding a new doctor with the best credentials. Your doctor should be certified by a medical organization. This means a test has been taken successfully.

About Victoria

Victoria Grove's interest in helping people to get better health care began years ago, first through her observations at work. Later, she became even more resolute after hearing many stories from people who had received ineffective treatment. Some had been turned away from medical providers with no help for their suffering. She has studied these issues and is working on a web site to serve as a resource for people who need help in this area.

Victoria worked in the health-care field for twenty-five years, first while attending the Universities of Iowa and Minnesota, then as a full-time clinic administrator, group problem- solving trainer and health-care management consultant.

She also spent time doing complex freelance work for an eminent psychologist. This led to the creation of a small business – Ducks On A Roll – which involved working with other professionals.

During the years 2003-2008, Victoria wrote and published poetry which resulted in several published poems, a listing in Who's Who in International Poetry in 2004 and 2012 and a second-place win in an international poetry-writing contest.

Victoria has received awards in the areas of academics, health care management and communication. Finding a challenge in identifying institutional problems and implementing effective solutions, she has been working on ways to help people navigate the complex health care system. Too many people are harmed by the medical system, which exists to help them. Communication is an area that is often implicated in unexpected poor results. Many of these errors can be avoided by using simple communication strategies. She is an advocate for improving health care outcomes.

If you would like to be on her mailing list, her e-mail address is: vgrove48_3@q.com. She will be able to contact you when her new web site is published.

References

"Buy this book! Victoria Grove is an expert in how communication affects healthcare as well as other issues in healthcare. She knows firsthand these issues and how to effectively solve problems we all experience."

~ Anne F. Kolar, M.D., *Child Psychiatrist*

"We all benefit from this book! Victoria Grove has extensive knowledge in the health care communications realm. She has been a passionate voice for the advancement of health care outcomes and I am pleased to have worked with her experience and integrity."

~ Susan Krtinch, R.N., *CRM*

"Experience in medical settings has given Victoria Grove unique insights into how patients can get better care for themselves by small changes in how they communicate with doctors and other health providers. She shares them with you in this chapter."

~ Leslie Yonce, Ph.D.

"I have known Ms. Grove for over thirty years. I have never failed to be struck by her insight into complex interpersonal situations, and her judgment is beyond compare."

~ W.G., Ph.D. - *Health Care Provider*

"Victoria is one of the brightest, hardest-working and most dedicated people I know."
~ B.G., M.D., Ph.D. – *former employer*

CHAPTER 6

TO ATTAIN EXCELLENCE – YOU MUST LEAVE MEDIOCRITY BEHIND

BY CHRIS BROWN

I want you to walk with me for a second. And take a little step into my life. You see, when I first started out you could say I was 'lost,' maybe 'unfocussed,' and certainly 'unsure' of my life's direction.

My parents are normal parents, my Dad worked in a factory for 25 years building cars. Now, I am incredibly proud of him as he is hugely passionate about his job, and does earn a good living from it. My Mam (that's what we say in the northeast of England) was an IT manager for a rather large American company and later started her own business. My grandparents are all of working class creed and worked incredibly hard all of their lives!

All of them instilled in me to be my very best and I'm thankful for that. The reason I mention my background to you is essentially because it's a normal or average background.

While nothing was 'handed to me on a plate,' my parents always 'busted their ass' for me and still do – and that's generally how parents are!

My first job when I left school was in McDonalds. Seems crazy, as it's a million miles from where I am now! I won't even buy a McDonalds for moral reasons now. But big or small, we all start somewhere. It was a bit of cash whilst I was at college.

From there, I finished college and got a job with Nissan, following in my father's footsteps (against his will). I always wanted to go to University, but just felt I need to get out into the 'real world' (later I realised most people get stuck in the 'real world') and earn some money.

I did earn a fair amount in the 15 months I spent there. In fact, it was around £30,000, which is a LOT of money for an 18-year-old kid. I remember being super proud of my Dad, everyone in the Factory had a great sense of respect for him and I quote, "he is one of the good guys in here." I guess my Dad is a natural-born leader, he just doesn't see it! I wish he did, maybe one day reading this he will!

Anyway, after spending 15 months there and loving it, I remember a guy who worked on my 'zone' saying to me, "Get out of here before the money gets you." It was like a slap in the face. That's what my Dad always said to me too. He only ever wanted it to be short-term thing.

Davy was the guy's name, he went on to say: "I say this because I care about you, I can see you have potential, you're a young boy in a man's world. You should be out enjoying yourself."

Damn! He was right. I remember I started trying to entertain my overactive mind by racing the man opposite me to build the same parts. (There were 'jigs' in which you placed and welded parts together, one man did the left hand side, the other did the right hand side). I'd wait for the man to start then race him. The funny thing is, the man didn't know I was racing him!

So yea, Davy was right. It was time to move on!

It was a 'ballsy' big move! Giving up a steady and regular income of £1,600 per month. For the life of a 'skint' student... (skint - UK slang for Broke)

And boy was I a 'skint' student!

Anyway, 3 years later I graduated with a BSc in Sports Coaching for Performance and Participation and moved to another city 3 hours away from where I grew up, not knowing a single soul.

I got qualified as a Personal Trainer and set up my 'business.' I say business, but it wasn't really, it was a Self-Employed 'JOB' - Just Over Broke.

I basically paid rent as a freelance agent within a gym. I had no clue about business then. In fact, I was the laziest person when it came to any kind of development. No reading, no courses. All I used to do was lounge around and play table tennis!

Then one day, I had a pretty big bust up with the 'manager.' I say 'manager' but she was far from a manager! In fact, what I learned from her that day taught me a valid lesson of how not to treat people.

The bust up ended in me having my contract terminated on the spot, and me losing each and everyone of my clients. That's when I realised I had no business.

In fact, not only that, but I had no family in the new area and one single friend. Other than that, nothing. That day was the 23rd of December. I decided that day, moving forward, I would never allow myself to be in that position again and this is where the story begins.

How did I take myself from broke, losing my job, having £640 in my bank, £600 of which I invested into a mentor knowing very well that was my money to 'live' for the next few weeks. I guess I always had a Warrior buried deep within my soul. It was only at this point I realised that and finally 'woke up.'

It's funny! I remember that day being of huge significance to my success so far!

Investing my last £600 into a mentor would strike the start of something I'd never imagined!

Which brings me to the seven habits that every modern day Warrior must possess! My mission through this article is to empower you with self-worth and vision to go and take EXACTLY what you want from life by giving first!

These habits are in no particular order of importance, as each element plays a vital role. Every Warrior realises the importance of this. They are an accumulation of experience through business, life and intense study and literally working with thousand's of people.

The one thing I want to stress before diving into this is that – *'Leaders are not born, they are created!'*

1. The Warrior understands that: Self-investment is the most powerful kind of investment. Investing in knowledge and future knowledge. Investing time as well as money into their future.

The Warrior will never settle or sit comfortably. They realise that there is always 'something else' to progress and move forward with. Imagine skiing up a very steep hill. Unless you continue to ski, one thing will happen. If you pause for a moment or sit around to 'enjoy the scenery' (relating to sitting in a comfort zone), you slide, …you slide backwards.

A Warrior understands that if they are to stop pressing forward and developing, they stop moving forward. They understand that life is a journey that never ends, and they continually push on the boundaries of 'ordinary' in order to create 'extra-ordinary things.'

2. Warriors are resilient. Warriors realise that resilience is key and that yes, sometimes, to move forward you must be knocked back, and that people will take digs and shots at you and will try and prevent you moving forward.

Not only that things don't always go in the favoured direction. The Warrior understands that when things don't move in the right direction, the Warrior possesses the 'foresight' to change and innovate. To re-create and re-build.

The Warrior understands that done is never done – and that everything requires constant change and innovation. As the great ancient Greek philosopher Heraclitus said: *"The only constant is change. Change is the only constant."*

Most people fail by creating something that 'worked' for a while, but when something or somebody pushes back, they don't have the resilience to withstand the pressure and then lack the foresight to innovate!

3. Warriors will always leave a legacy that far outlives their life. You may think of many 'Warriors' leaders of the past, that are still quoted to this day, …ten, twenty or a hundred years later. They are quoted because they had a message to spread, a purpose on the planet, and decided to commit to making a legacy that far outlives them.

The Warrior is driven by purpose and attitude – the right attitude to deliver meaningful purpose and achieve. The legacy builds and people want to be part of the legacy and will often help to craft and create a legacy.

Warrior legacy carries values that will never be over-turned. The Warrior is VERY sure of who they are and what is important to them and will never 'sell-out' nor will they go against who they are or what they value.

Warriors will always "push on the ocean" and aim to create a ripple that will touch many lives in a positive, impactful way. Warriors are strong-minded and focused.

4. Warriors always strive for Excellence. They understand that excellence is not always perfection. The Warrior will always give everything they have and more, in order to be the VERY best person they can be!

A Warrior will never accept second best from themselves, and always inspires those around them to strive for excellence in themselves. Good is not good enough. The Warrior will always aim to be the VERY best at their craft and strive constantly and push to be better.

The Warrior understands and adopts this phrase. *"Leader of One, Leader of Many, If you Can't Lead One, You Can't Lead Any."*

5. The Warrior is 'Real' and lives a life based around Honesty and Integrity both with themselves and others.

The Warrior has the unique ability to be 100% honest with themselves. A Warrior will ALWAYS admit when they have been wrong in the past, and even if it means moving towards excellence, will accept that decisions and choices they have made could have been better at the time. And sometimes, more often than not, the decision they made was wrong, or at the time was right with the knowledge they possessed at that particular time.

Warriors also accept 100% responsibility for EVERY occurrence in their life, even if they feel others have been malicious or are at fault.

The Warrior will never blame others. Warriors always find the responsibility within themselves and take the right action moving forward towards their vision.

The Warrior understands this phrase deeply: *"If you're part of the problem, you're part of the solution."*

6. A Warrior will always build a community of followers through the power of their communication. The Warrior attracts people to share their values, purpose and mission. The Warrior will often do this non-intentionally, but such is the power of their message that people follow, engage and be part of the mission.

The Warrior is empathetic with their community and will constantly strive to inspire the community to achieve success in whatever direction it may be! The Warrior understands the importance of purpose within people and will always do their best to find purpose and bring purpose out of people.

More importantly, the Warrior understands self-purpose and will inspire through the audacious actions of themselves.

7. The Warrior possesses an amazing Sense of Vision and will always plan the vision. The Warrior knows exactly what they want!

It's not by chance that the Warrior will strive for excellence in life! The Warrior will always visualise the future plans, understanding that visualisation is a powerful technique.

The Warrior understands the power of the sub-conscious mind and right brain, and will program their sub-conscious to take the right actions towards their end-visualisation.

Often, the Warrior will do this in a creative manner – drawing, mind-mapping and plotting in a very visual and kinesthetic way.

The Warrior is a true renegade, and will often visualise very abstract and different routes going against the *status-quo* of what is normal, and will fully persevere through the majority of people telling them what they're doing is 'wrong' or 'can't be done.'

The Warrior stays true to the vision and understands the power of persevering. The Warrior understands that the line between Success and Failure is very close. The failures just can't visualise how close. The Warrior understands that every triumph happens over Adversity.

I want you to take the time out now from whatever you may be doing and just think. Think about, first of all, the key to any progress – understanding the 'blockage.'

What is the one thing that is holding you back from getting what you want? Write that down on a piece of paper. Remember just because you are where you are now, doesn't mean you're going to end up there!

Sometimes we feel as though we have pushed so far into one direction that there's no turning back. I have done this so many times in the past. So many times it's unreal!

However, becoming a true leader and becoming a Warrior, you understand that no matter how far you have come in one direction, it doesn't mean you can't simply stop and turn around and start over. Many people have this 'notion' that they're too old, or too qualified in one area, or nobody would want them in this area. The Warrior understands that these are all excuses for not going and getting out of your comfort zone.

Imagine walking around all day everyday with a hula-hoop constantly attached around your feet. That is your comfort zone. Just close your eyes and visualise that for a second.

Now, with one foot step out of the hula hoop, and then, then with the second foot step out of the hula hoop. Go against what you believe to be impossible and make it possible. It really sounds easy, doesn't it? Well, I got news for you... It is.

Remember whether you believe you can or you believe you can't, you're right! The only person holding you back is you, and your self-limiting beliefs. Why would you do that? Why would you allow yourself to prevent you from moving forward? I promise you; it's as simple as making a decision and stepping out of the metaphorical hula-hoop that you're trapped in.

Now it is simple, but it isn't easy, not everybody has the audacity or courage to be the Warrior.

However the Warrior begins to be uncomfortable at being comfortable! It's really as simple as that! The Journey is never an easy one, The Warrior battles through deep, dangerous forests with unknown beasts, but the Warrior also experiences all of the things that those people not willing to test the unknown, haven't.

The Warrior lives. With each breath, the Warrior understands it's one closer to death. Warriors understand their own mortality. Make the rest of your life the best of your life, stop procrastinating and worrying about things that may never occur. Visualise, dream in colour and venture into the unknown. Take risks and just trust your own intuition. You have it in you. You have the ability to do whatever you want.

Leave mediocrity behind you, strive for excellence!

About Chris

Chris Brown is making a name for himself as the UK's Young and Hot Speaker in Self-Empowerment and Leadership – fusing his knowledge of Nutrition and Training in a way nobody else has before.

Chris was highlighted as part of the 'World Fitness Elite' and featured in USA Today and also The Times as a Leading trainer in the World. He founded his primary Business Fitness Camp Academy in late 2010, and has since grown it to 15 different locations within the UK.

The Fitness Camp Academy's mission statement is: "To Inspire and Create Positive Lasting Change in the Lives of Our Members and Commitment To Being the Best Part of Their Day EACH and EVERY Day."

Chris is a qualified Executive Business Leadership Coach and Accelerated Learning Coach. He fuses these skills with training and nutrition to help people Self-Empower themselves and craft and create the Life that they truly desire! Strength, Vigour, Courage, Health, Honesty, Integrity and Commitment to Excellence are all highly important values to Chris and he helps to instill these within the lives of the people he coaches!

He believes in the 'Warrior' mentality and utilising the habits of a Warrior. A quote that has major resonation with Chris is:

> Out of every one hundred men, ten shouldn't even be there, eighty are just targets, nine are the real fighters, and we are lucky to have them, for they make the battle. Ah, but the one, One is a warrior, and he will bring the others back ~ Heraclitus

Chris believes everybody has the power to be the Warrior to utilise a Self-Empowered Lifestyle taking control of their choices and decisions that lead to being healthy, happy and fulfilled. "Leader of ONE, Leader of Many, if You can't Lead One, You Can't Lead Any."

Chris is highly successful in Business and at such a young age of 25, he has managed to figure out EXACTLY what he wants from life. This is something that many people never figure out. He is a true inspirational leader that can help you get exactly what you want out of your body, mind, life and business.

For more information, head over to: www.purposeoftheweek.com
Or call +447824331590

CHAPTER 7

RETIRE WITH GRACE

BY CHARLES J BROCK II,
PhD, LUTCF, RFC, CSA

Have you ever built a home or decided you wanted to build the home of your dreams? Without any kind of excavation, building, electrical, plumbing, masonry experience or knowledge of building codes, would you simply run out to the store and begin purchasing lumber, light fixtures, carpet, and windows? Of course you wouldn't, because you understand the need for the help of professionals to turn your dreams into reality. You know that a blueprint is the first step to putting the pieces in place properly.

The same holds true with your money. Without a financial blueprint, you run the risk of owning financial products that don't accomplish your goals, fit or work well together. The result: your money might not enable you to live your dreams. Unlike a room that turns out to be too small, or a kitchen with too few electrical outlets, you may not be aware that your financial plan won't work for you as you hoped. A *RETIREMENT AR-CHITECT* can assist you in creating and implementing your custom-designed financial blueprint.

WHAT IS A <u>RETIREMENT ARCHITECT?</u>

A Retirement Architect is a professional who specializes in helping retirees and soon-to-be retirees build strong financial portfolios. Portfolios that, first and foremost, provide *safety* and the highest, most *Tax-Favored* income stream that *cannot be outlived*. Much like the more conventional architect who designs and supervises the construction of buildings, a retirement architect designs a financial plan that will be flexible, effective, and strong—based on the individual client's needs— and then supervises the implementation of the plan.

When a retirement architect meets with a client, he or she discusses the needs and expectations of the client. Every person is different, and it's important to come up with a long-term financial planning solution that is achievable and effective for each individual client. A 60-year-old single woman, for example, has very different needs from a 75-year-old couple. In addition to providing financial planning assistance, a retirement architect can help with wealth and asset protection planning, as well as showing people how to tax-efficiently transfer their assets to the next generation.

A retirement architect emphasizes and specializes in asset **Preservation and Distribution**. Retirement Architects work to relieve their clients of worry and help them overcome their greatest fear: outliving their money. Just as important, they can help their clients understand the three phases of money and provide them with the information and guidance needed to make informed decisions and, if needed, a shift in perspective.

THE SHIFT IN PERSPECTIVE

You've worked hard all your life. You've saved and sacrificed and grown a sizable retirement fund as a result. Now, however, the future doesn't look so certain. Many of you have seen as much as 40% of your retirement funds disappear in a matter of months. And it's not because you were unlucky or uninformed. It's because you were still investing in an accumulation mindset aka "paycheck mode", as you have most of your life, when what is required is a shift in perspective.

There are three phases of money in everyone's financial life: accumulation, preservation and distribution. The first phase, accumulation, is what I call "paycheck mode". During your pre-retirement working years your paycheck is what puts food on your table, clothes on your back and gas in your tank. It can also become an investment mindset as well. Taking investment risk does not affect your lifestyle during your paycheck years. When the market goes up, your broker or advisor calls to say "Look what a great job I did for you!" When it goes down (and it always does at some point), you call your broker who (if he takes your call), says, "I don't have any control over the market. But hang in there – it'll come back" or something like "It's not a loss until you sell, and since you don't need the money right now there is no need to take any losses."

It doesn't matter who your financial advisor is – the last time I checked, no one had a crystal ball that works! Even if your advisor talked as though he or she could look into the future, we all know they can't. Most brokers infer that the past has some connection with the future. It's fundamental to their investment philosophy; they're constantly hawking the story of historical returns. The question I pose to you is what connection does yesterday have with tomorrow? The answer is: NONE AT ALL! The darling of Wall Street today probably won't be the darlings tomorrow... and most likely won't be in five years. That's the fallacy of investing in the Wall Street *Casino*.

The story your advisor or broker wanted you to believe is that the market will climb back out of the hole and continue to go up. In years long past, this may have been true. But those were the years when you had plenty of something that's not so abundant today if you are close to, or in retirement ... **time**. Keep in mind that there is a reason why the last ten years are known on Wall Street as the 'Lost Decade.'

When you've got that paycheck coming in, you can wait for the market to go back up. But now that you're retired, things are different. That workday paycheck no longer exists and you still need cash flow. We call it your 'retirement paycheck'. If you maintain your investments in stocks and bonds, your money is at the whim of the market. I don't know anybody who wants to eat one month and starve the next!

During the working and investment years, most of us use a process called "dollar cost averaging." This strategy says that if you put an equal amount of money in an investment on a regular basis, buying some of the assets high and some low and averaging the costs in the middle, then if you sell any stocks, bonds, or mutual funds above the middle or mean price, you'll make a profit. When you are accumulating assets in pre-retirement, this is not a bad investment philosophy.

However, if you make withdrawals in a fluctuating market, it's called *reverse* dollar cost averaging, and it works just as effectively on a NEG-ATIVE basis. If you are pulling a fixed amount of money out of an asset that goes up and down, you are going to reduce your total account value fast - **too fast.**

Once you retire, the pot of money you've spent the last forty years putting together has to last you the rest of your life. It wasn't so long ago that people retired at sixty-five and died at sixty-five and-a-half. They didn't need much of a plan! But today people are living well into their nineties and sometimes well over age one hundred. With longevity on the rise, you need a plan that absolutely, contractually, guarantees income for as long as you live, not just as long as the money lasts.

Income is the only important thing in retirement. It's not net worth. It's not the number at the bottom of your financial statement. It's what's coming in the front door as a retirement paycheck that now puts food on the table and clothes on your back, (not to mention keeping the roof in good repair) and hopefully assuring all the additional perks of the good life you've worked so hard to enjoy in retirement.

So how do you create retirement income? By finding the right retirement architect to help you design the best possible retirement plan, in writing, created by an experienced team, including a group of highly-credentialed retirement planning specialists, CPAs, and attorneys.

THE <u>RETIREMENT</u> INVESTMENT PERSPECTIVE

As you near and enter retirement, your investment mindset must change from accumulation to one of preservation and/or distribution. This calls for a TRUE understanding of investment Safety vs. Risk and how to capture the best of both worlds. Mark Twain put it best when he said, "I am not as much interested in a return on my money, as I am a return **of** my money". Although this quote has often been attributed (erroneously) to Will Rodgers, it has become the retirees' creed and the true definition of safe investments.

Let's have a look at what safety vs. risk or, put another way, **Protection vs. Potential,** looks like. When you think of safe investments the first thing that should come to mind is **NO CHANCE OR POTENTIAL FOR LOSS!**

There are three primary sources for these types of safe or protected investments:

1. Banks – CDs
2. Government – US Treasures
3. Insurance Companies – Fixed Annuities.

These types of investments all have the following common characteristics:

1. Liquidity

2. The principal is guaranteed

3. Interest is guaranteed

4. The term is guaranteed

5. No or low fees

Safe or protected investments such as these do come with strings attached, however, such as low returns and penalties for early withdrawal. In today's market the potential returns over the next twelve months may only range from 0-3%.

That's the good and bad of these types of investments:

- The good – no chance for loss;
- The bad – modest potential for growth.

It's easy to understand why these types of investments are not very good accumulation options. They are and always will be thought of as only one thing, the **safe** place to put your money.

Could this be why most brokers never bring them up in their conversations with retirees? Could it be that most Wall Street types think in terms of potential growth and accumulation and **not** about safety? I'm sure the fact that these safe vehicles pay such low commissions never entered their minds. Personally I would hate to think that a broker might be more interested in commissions than the safety of their clients' money.

Now that we have opened the Pandora's Box of risk, let's review. Question: *Where are most retirees and soon-to-be retirees told to invest their money?*

Answer: *Investments with the potential for growth! Or, as I like to call it, the RISK MARKET.*

What types of investments might you find in the Risk Market?

- Variable Annuities

- Hedge Funds and Mutual Funds, Stocks, Options

- Bonds (Corporate, Government and Munis)

- Real Estate and REITS

- Limited Partnerships, Commodities, Futures

ANY INVESTMENT THAT HAS THE POTENTIAL FOR <u>LOSS.</u>

To be fair, these types of investments do have advantages for the younger investor:

1. Potential for growth

2. Liquidity (with exceptions)

3. Favorable tax treatment (this could diminish considerably starting in 2013)

4. Upside potential of 8-12%

Now let's look at why accumulation or growth potential investments are not a very good choice for the preservation or income-minded retiree:

1. Moderate to high Fees for both acquisition and management.

2. Principal is NOT guaranteed.

3. Interest/earnings are NOT guaranteed.

4. Term is generally open-ended.

5. Need TIME to be effective-how much?

6. Downside loss potential. (How much did **you** lose in 2008? Insert that number here.)

So, as a retiree or soon-to-be retiree, you think you can't afford safety because you have to make a high return on your money; but at the same time you are unable to suffer the losses associated with the risk usually necessary for potential growth. So what can you do?

Maybe it's time to take a look at a type of investment that is very seldom discussed: one that has most of the upside potential and little if any of the downside risk.

PROTECTION AND POTENTIAL
OR
THE BEST OF BOTH WORLDS

Hybrid investments link protection and safety with the potential for growth. First and foremost they start with principal protection. Although they are linked to an external market index such as the S&P500, they are NOT invested directly in the market.

A few of the Investments in this category include:
- Treasury Inflation-Protected Securities (TIPS)
- Equity-Linked CDs
- I-Bonds
- Fixed Indexed Annuities

United States Treasury Inflation-Protected Securities (TIPS) are marketable securities whose principal is adjusted by changes in the Consumer Price Index (CPI). With inflation (a rise in the index), the principal increases. With deflation (a drop in the index), the principal decreases. Since the interest rate is fixed, and it is applied to the adjusted principal the interest payments can vary from one period to the next.

At maturity of a TIPS, you receive the adjusted principal or the original principal, whichever is greater. TIPS are issued in terms of 5, 10 and 30 years.

An **Equity-Linked CD** is an FDIC-insured certificate of deposit that ties the rate of return to the performance of a stock index such as the S&P 500. The terms for calculation of interest on these CDs vary from institution to institution. They are typically issued for a term of five years.

I-Bonds are Treasury bonds that pay a fixed rate of interest as well as another layer of interest that varies with the current inflation rate, as measured by the CPI. The inflation adjustment is made twice a year, in May and November. I-Bonds reach their final maturity 30 years after issuance. I-Bonds incur penalties if redeemed within five years of purchase.

A **Fixed Indexed Annuity** (also known as Equity-indexed annuity or simply an indexed annuity) is a type of tax-deferred annuity whose credited interest is linked to an equity index — typically the S&P 500 or other international indexes. It guarantees a minimum interest rate (typically 1-3%) over the term of the contract and protects against a loss of principal. The returns may be higher depending on the performance of the index it is linked to. The guarantees in the contract are backed by the strength of the insurance company. The companies are called legal reserve insurance companies because the states have stringent requirements about the amount of reserves they must maintain to cover their obligations.. The objective of purchasing an equity-indexed annuity is to realize potentially greater gains than those provided by CDs, money markets or bonds, while still protecting principal. Through the addition of what are known as riders, such as a Guaranteed Minimum Income Benefit, credited interest rates can compound in the income account at a rate as high as 7%. This does not even take into account the bonus many contracts offer.

THE BOTTOM LINE

The bottom line is that the assurance of a known future value that can be converted into an income stream of money each year can make projections of one's future cash flows less problematic. The reality of retirement is that it really is all about **Cash-Flow**.

The chart below, of the three investment worlds of money, should help bring your retirement perspective into focus.

Three WORLDS

This is an illustration only and is not intended to be a projection or prediction of current or future performance of any specific product. Product features, limitations and availability vary by state. Guarantees are subject to the financial strength and claims-paying ability of the issuing insurance company. A surrender of and/or withdrawals from an annuity contract may be subject to taxation as ordinary income and if taken prior to age 59½ may be subject to a 10% IRS penalty tax. Individual should consult with a professional specializing in the areas of tax, legal, accounting or investments regarding the applicability of this information to his/her situation.

Now that you have reviewed this chart, I have one final question.

As a retiree or soon-to-be retiree, where do you think your money should be?

Make sure you connect with a properly credentialed and experienced retirement architect to assist in building your financial house of security. People of all ages and socioeconomic classes can benefit from consulting a retirement architect. It's never too early to start planning for the future, and by working with a financial expert, people can avoid a lot of pitfalls and mistakes that could cost them money.

Financial planning includes saving and accumulating money for retirement, college, and big expenses.

Retirement Planning is all about managing **existing** wealth effectively so that it will generate interest income and continue to grow while focusing on "safety" preservation and long-term distribution through tax-advantaged concepts such as the Super Roth Solution.

If your advisor cannot explain the Super Roth Solution concept, feel free to contact me at: chuckb@gracetax.com.

About Chuck

Charles J Brock II, PhD, LUTCF, RFC, CSA is Vice President of the Grace Advisory Group, headquartered in Fort Myers, FL, with offices throughout Southwest and Central Florida.

He is a nationally-recognized retirement income architect who is regularly sought out by the media, and is seen on TV and regularly heard on radio stations throughout Central and Southwest Florida.

Chuck has been providing comprehensive wealth management for affluent individuals and families, with an emphasis on personalized service, for over 20 years, and has consulted for such firms as Merrill Lynch, Morgan Stanley and Prudential.

Among his numerous credentials, he not only has a PhD in Economics, he is also a Life Underwriter Training Council Fellow, Registered Financial Consultant and a Certified Senior Advisor.

He also has the unique distinction of not only being an Admiral in the Texas Navy, but also a Kentucky Colonel, both honors awarded by the Governors of those states.

At Grace Advisory Group he oversees a team—of legal, tax, accounting, financial and insurance experts— that specializes in building financial plans that emphasize safety, while reducing taxes and providing a steady revenue stream that its clients cannot outlive. They help individual and business clients establish sophisticated, yet easy to understand, solutions for protecting and preserving wealth, while minimizing tax exposure. For more information on how they may be able to help you, visit: www.gracetax.com.

CHAPTER 8

MARKETING/ PROMOTIONS

BY JAMES STUBBS

Marketing and Promotions is the key component that your business must do consistently in order to keep your business alive. I've been behind the scenes promoting events and parties for over 20 years now, and have seen the best and the worse when it comes to the energy and finances a business will put into Marketing & Promotions.

Some business owners think just because they start a business, people will come. How do people, besides your family and friends, know that your business even exists? Are you even aware of how your competitors are standing out or how they seem to have a constant flow of traffic to their business?

My Five P's...

Most marketing specialists would begin their discussion with the first four P's:

(1) Product – does it bring value; is it good?

(2) Price – is it too high or too low? Do your homework.

(3) Place – is it convenient for the customer to purchase?

(4) Promotion – is all about how and where you publicize.

(5) My 5th 'P' I want to share is 'Positioning'… This is how I suggest you stay creative and relevant and build awareness every time you

put out a new product or service. Your Positioning strategy is the image you want to draw in the mind of the potential customer/lead.

The public must be aware that your products or services exist. You must make your presence felt in areas where your buyers can discover you. Inasmuch as you hate loads of hefty commercials during the Super Bowl games, those advertisements are meant to catch the attention of the billions of people watching the game. Ask yourself, how many new people on a daily basis can you get your brand in front of?

There are two ways of promoting your business. You can create awareness through offline and online efforts. Offline methods are traditional marketing efforts that involve physically bringing the advertising product or service closer to the buyer. This can be done through an actual sales demo, via radio and television commercials, newsletters, flyers, tee shirts, and a host of offline events – including giveaways with your company website address, special events, contests, community service and parties.

Just because the Internet is the hottest and latest means of communication, it does not mean that offline marketing and promotions are dead. Trust me, it is not. People still shop in malls and grocery stores; go to plays, concerts, getaway trips, school, church, clubs, sporting events, etc. These people are also your potential customers, so you must always have marketing material available at any of these venues in order to capture attention and get them online to your email list. The bottom line - it's always your job to get new leads onto your mailing list. The money is in the list building. Once you get the email/mailing address, you now have the chance to build a lasting relationship and offer your products or services for the lifetime of that relationship.

OFFLINE & ONLINE PROMOTIONS
WORK TOGETHER...

Last year my girlfriend decided she was going to get involved with a Network Marketing group. In order to bring awareness and local attention to her new venture, I talked her into promoting two events, in one day. The first event was a Seminar that was to start on a Saturday @ 1pm at a hotel ballroom. The second event was a party that was going to be held at the same hotel ballroom but starting @ 9pm that evening.

I had 30,000 professional flyers made up promoting the Network Marketing seminar on one side and the party promotions on the other side of the flyer. On both sides of the flyer there were clear bold and legible directions to go online and leave your name and email in order to receive complimentary (free admission) tickets for both events.

Now bear in mind, in order to promote the events, I was aware of every major event and party going on in a 10-mile radius of where my girlfriend's event was going to being held, for the entire month prior to her event date. One major local event that was happening on the same day prior to her party was a large-scale parade. I knew where and when to have my promotional street team, handing out flyers at all times.

Because she was new to the Network Marketing group, I told her it was in her best interest to link up with someone in the Network marketing company with higher rankings to do the presentation at the seminar in order to get people to join under her so that she can start off in the Network marketing company with a bang. Good positioning strategy.

The Network Marketing group seminar was presented as the newest and hottest thing to join in order for her leads to want to join and cash in as early as possible. My girlfriend received hundreds of leads from directing the people to go online and enter their email address from the offline flyer promotions. Two hundred twenty two people actually showed up for the seminar.

Once the people downloaded their complimentary ticket to the venues, on the fine print for the party ticket it also indicated a 2 drink minimum – all expiring @ 10pm. Many people were trying to get in the party before 10pm with the doors opening @ 9pm. With this strategy, the party was a hit from the beginning. At 11pm, I doubled the door entry fee since the line was wrapped around the block.

By 12:30am the party capacity was at its maximum leaving crowds of people outside not able to get into the party. Knowing this might happen, I gave out flyers made up in advance, to these people for an event I scheduled two weeks later. On the flyer of course it led the people to go online to enter their email address for complimentary tickets.

The Bottom line was 2 major and successful events in one day. Thirty-eight people signed up that day under the Network Marketing group.

That's huge for a beginner. Because hundreds of people joined the email list there was still plenty of opportunity to build the relationship for future sales.

The profit from the party was $18,222. Over 1,000 people showed up. Do not sleep on offline promotions! People like meeting business owners personally because it makes them feel important. Attend events where you can personally shake hands with your potential buyers. Event promotions bring awareness, leave the image of community ties and can bring you new leads consistently.

Boost your networking efforts online. I've met so many business owners and authors who do not have a web presence. That leaves a lot of money on the table, and a lot of people that need your products and services are being denied because they do not know you exist.

DEVELOPING YOUR SYSTEMS

Today, in order to survive the competition, you must have a web presence (website/blog) and be constantly learning new ways of Marketing and Promotions. You can hire a professional web developer from elance.com or guru.com for a reasonable price.

Develop your website with interesting information so that customers can spend a lot of time exploring your site. You can add relevant articles, success stories, company events with photos and more. You can even create step-by-step guides on how to make full use of your product. Add freebies such as downloadable newsletters, reports, e-books and other types of gifts. Make your customers feel that they are getting so much value from your product. Keep your customer interested and they will keep going back to your website.

Become an author and create your own book. This positions you as an expert and people will look at you as the go-to person for relevant solutions to their problems. As an author of an e-book, you can market your e-book online in many different ways that can bring in multiple streams of income as well as many new leads.

As an author, this also positions you to be called on for speaking engagements – which adds on another stream of income and brings on another avenue of new potential leads. Whenever you speak, make sure you record the sessions. This provides you with more products to either give away, use to package up as membership only products, or even just to sell to bring in more leads.

There are unlimited amounts of online promotions that you can do to market and promote your brand on a daily basis. Learn and implement them one by one: email marketing, article marketing, video marketing and Social Media marketing just for starters. It will get easier once you learn how to automate a lot of these efforts.

a. Email marketing is essential and it's a low-cost way to generate more sales after you establish a relationship and become credible with your email list. Always use a variety of methods to build your email list.

b. Article marketing can bring you tons of traffic to your website. Write an article 3 to 5 times a week and send it out to a minimum of ten Article Directories.

c. Video marketing is valuable. Create a series of 'how to' videos and package them for viewers to watch on your membership site. For every article you write, read and record them onto an audio program, include seven bullet points onto a PowerPoint slide, and use Sony Movie Studio to put the audio and slides all together. Start to build your videos. Submit your videos to a minimum of ten video sites. Continue being consistent to drive traffic to your site using this video marketing strategy.

d. Promoting on social media is of course one way you should not leave out of your promotions strategies. A big factor in successful Social Media marketing is knowing who your target audience is and how to reach them. You should know your target audience (age group, gender, ethnic group, hobbies, etc.) so you can determine how to reach them.

Facebook and Google advertising, if done right, can be a very lucrative strategy using cost per click (CPC). You, as the advertiser, determine the CPC for the ad. The formula for cost per click is: CPC = cost / clicks.

Example: For a given campaign over a given period, an ad was clicked 100 times. The campaign cost $40. CPC = $40 / 100. CPC = $0.40 - The average CPC was $0.40 per click.

IS THERE MONEY IN THE SYSTEMS?

Whether you are just starting out in business or you currently are looking for more ways to generate growth, remember a few important things:

1) You must master your niche.

2) You must know your target audience.

3) You must discover your audience's issues and problems via surveying or simple questions.

4) You must create solutions for your audience with a variety of products.

Let's look at just the few different modalities I've mentioned already and see how easy it is to generate $200,000 a year.

Here are examples for the System:

- Create an e-book and sell 5 e-books a day for $37.

- Create a 4 CD set audio program and sell 3 per day for $97.

- Create a membership subscription training program with your 'how to' videos and deliver new content monthly to keep the subscribers engaged - $49 a month per membership @ 50 people.

- Conduct a Live Seminar once per year getting a minimum of 50 people @ $200.

Here's the math: (from above example)

$66,600 a year (E-books)

$104,760 a year (Audio CD's)

$29,400 a year (Membership Subscription)

$10,000 a year (Live Seminar)

Total = $210,760 a Year.

Now is the time to give valuable solutions to your customers and move forward creating the business and life you want while doing so.

Blessings!
James Stubbs
G hop Promotions

About James

James Stubbs

Alexandria, VA

G hop Promotions

James-Stubbs.com

James Stubbs has been known for Marketing & Promoting Events and Parties in the New York City area for over 20 years. From Faith-based events to multi-level marketing events, Club promotions, get-away trips, Comedy shows and a host of many other entertainment and network marketing venues.

To learn more about James Stubbs, and how to Market and promote online and offline, you can visit his blog at: **www.james-stubbs.com**.

CHAPTER 9

HONOR: AN ANCIENT SECRET THAT LEVERAGES YOUR BIGGEST ASSET

BY HARRISON WILDER

You already know that focus, hard work and determination can take you far. You probably know that what you believe about yourself is the only real limit to your potential. But do you know that your biggest asset actually has nothing to do with you and your abilities? In fact, the biggest asset available to you…is in others! Wrapped up in the relationships around you are years of wisdom, knowledge and experience. Leveraging that asset means learning the secret to open what's inside those relationships and making it accessible to you.

FRUSTRATED WITH LACK OF SUCCESS

I happen to be one of the most independent people on the planet. I have a natural tendency to believe that I know best about pretty much everything. As a result, it never occurred to me growing up to look outside myself for answers or information.

I remember one particular occasion; I was helping my dad with a project around the house. He sent me to the tool shed to find something he needed. I darted across the yard, excited to be able to help, and stopped in the doorway of the tool shed. I started looking around for the tool he requested. It was probably after ten minutes of frantically searching, feeling like a failure that I couldn't find the tool, worried that I would disappoint my dad, before it finally hit me…I had no idea what the tool looked like!

Years later, I reflected back on this experience. I recalled the frustration and the disappointment I felt in myself, and I realized that my perspective was completely skewed. I was just a child. I wasn't supposed to have all the answers…and my father, he knew exactly what that tool looked like. All I needed to have done was ask, and he would have been delighted to teach me what I needed to know to get the job done.

This may seem like a ridiculous childhood example, but chances are you're in the exact same situation. You may feel frustrated for not having realized certain dreams, but the truth is you just don't know everything you need to know to get there. There is no reason for you to feel discouraged. You just need to tap into the knowledge of people around you.

AN ANCIENT TRADITION

The secret to tapping into this hidden reservoir is the ancient practice of honor. I call it ancient both because it has been in practice since the beginning of time, and because it is presently quite counter-cultural. In fact, the practice of honor is almost completely lost on our generation – simply because we don't understand it or the benefits it can offer. Our celebration of independence and individuality has torn away at what allows us to share and build on the successes of others. We feel responsible to achieve success on our own and don't value what is given to us from parents, bosses, mentors and those just a little further along than us. Honor recognizes that the people around us are valuable resources to be treasured and appreciated.

There is a Thai tradition that illustrates honor very well. The Thai culture is well known for its reverence of parents and elders. In the ceremony of Wai Khru, students pay homage to their teachers to express their gratitude and to formalize the student-teacher relationship. The student recognizes the role of the teacher and submits to his instruction. The *wai khru* chant, which expresses respect for the teachers, ends with 'an ask'…for the teachers' blessing of their studies[1].

---

1 http://en.wikipedia.org/wiki/Wai_khru

This tradition demonstrates a belief that the posture of the student is supremely important to facilitate the learning process. It shows there is a relationship between honor and the blessing. The students value the teacher and are positioned to receive what the teacher has to offer.

The practice of honor is all about positioning you to receive the blessing…the wealth of knowledge, and wisdom others have to offer.

Five ways to practice honor and position yourself to receive its blessing:

1. Think *Multi-Generational*

We've created a culture that celebrates the success of the individual. We exalt the image of a "self-made" man and write off the contributions of others as "trust-fund babies" who had everything delivered to them on a silver platter. The truth, though, is that the challenges that face us are too big for one generation. While we may set in motion great solutions for the future, it will be up to future generations to finish the work. And, we're going to have to rely on the experience of previous generations as we develop our solutions. A more prosperous future won't be the result of one generation rising to the challenge, but many generations coming together, building one on the other.

This is true for us as individuals as well. I've personally spent too many years trying to build a great future for my wife and kids on my own. I'm discovering that my success doesn't begin and end with my contribution. What's really important is my ability to receive from others, build on it, and to pass along what I've learned to those who come after me. In the big picture, the relationship between generations becomes the key building block for the future.

When we see things that way, we automatically elevate our starting platform beyond our own abilities. Our potential is significantly increased just because of a change in perspective. What valuable relationships are around you? What if their accomplishments were not a threat to your success but a compliment? What if you could build on what they've learned and achieve things they never dreamed of? That's the power of honor!

Its antithesis is quite ridiculous: What if every generation learned every lesson for themselves? What if we never passed along successes or failures from one generation to the other? Society would never advance. It would reset itself every 70 years or so! It's the same with you. The first step toward receiving the blessing of honor is a perspective change. See your life as an extension of generations that have preceded you. Build on their success. Learn from their failures. Discover a future far brighter than you or they could have imagined.

2. *Value* Input

There is an ancient Hebrew text that dates back as far as Moses. It says,

"Honor your father and your mother…so that you may live long and that it may go well with you…" [2]

Using a loose understanding of the words "father and mother," the text shows a relationship between our success and the posture we keep toward parents (teachers, bosses, mentors, leaders, etc.). The ancient Hebrew word for "honor" actually means, "to make weighty." Imagine a group of wrestlers all lined up in a row. They are equal in skill, training, and heart. Then, in your mind, pick out one and add 15 pounds of muscle to him. Now he stands out from the crowd. All other things being equal, as the weightier wrestler, he's likely to win a match against any of the other competitors. He is respected, feared, distinguished. He's unique. He's been given special attention. I interpret this to mean that when we decide to honor someone, we "add weight" to their lives. We consider them unique, prefer them, give them special attention, value them, listen to them and respect them.

Who in your life is "weightier" than others? They're not like a peer to you. Their input is sought out and respected above what others have to say. We need relationships like this if we're going to make the most out of life. Unleashing the power of honor means seeking out relationships where you really value and weigh heavily the input they bring.

Usually we don't like to value another person until they've earned and maintained our respect. But a word of caution, that posture may cause you to miss out on a valuable relationship. If you wait around for a perfect person to help instruct and guide you, you'll be waiting for a long time. I'm not saying to open yourself up to just anyone, but once you decide to engage in an honoring relationship, go ahead and commit. Decide: *This person is valuable.* They don't always necessarily deserve it. They don't need to earn it. It's not contingent on their actions. It's a

---

2. Deuteronomy 5:1

posture you've taken so that you can learn from them.

3. Assume a *Submissive* Posture

Submission. I don't know anyone who likes this word…me included! But it's impossible to take full advantage of honor without a submissive posture. But, we're adults right? We're responsible for our own lives. Why should we submit to others? I have two questions I ask to help me determine when honor is calling me to submit to someone else:

A.) *"Who is responsible for the actions that need to be made?"*
For instance, if an employer asks you to do a certain task relating to the company, even if you don't like it, honoring his or her position as your employer would mean not only being respectful in your response, but also being obedient to carry out the request. In this situation, your employer is the responsible authority in the work environment, not you. This holds true for relationships with all kinds of authorities (church leadership, government, teachers, HOA board, etc.). In their respective realms, they are responsible for our actions and us. Within those realms, we honor them by being submissive.

If you can learn to apply this test inside your relationships with people of authority, you'll see people in those positions start to trust you with more responsibility. They will open up their internal supply of wisdom, knowledge and even their relationships with you. There is an even deeper principle at play here, though, one that says "you reap what you sow." If you'll assume a submissive posture to people who have authority, you'll find that the people you lead will take the same posture toward you.

B.) *"Do I want to submit this area of my life to this person?"*
Even when we're ultimately responsible for certain choices in our lives, there are times that we enter into relationships where we temporarily defer to others. In those situations, honor may mean submitting to others even when they're not ultimately responsible for our actions. For instance, if you engage a personal trainer to help you become physically fit, you're wise to obey what they ask of you…even when you don't feel like it or understand why. You've deferred to them because of their expertise. You may engage in this kind of relationship with a

parent, pastor, mentor, accountability partner or someone who is apprenticing you. It may be temporary over just a little area of your life, or a long-term relationship that spans many areas of influence.

I engaged in this kind of relationship when I was about to ask my wife to marry me. It was very important to me that her father give his approval before we were engaged. Call me old-fashioned, but I believe there are times when we can experience a greater degree of blessing if we will honor the right people at the right time. Honoring her father in this instance was taking the next step of our relationship and submitting it to him. We were both out of the house, both very responsible for our own lives and choices, but we were committed to submit this decision to him.

This doesn't mean that you have to be a "yes-person" – never challenging anyone's perspective. Even in healthy submissive relationships, you should look for opportunities to voice an opinion and give feedback. Your role in your organization may even be to bring a dissenting point of view. Honor, however, will test your willingness to submit to another and keep your posture in check.

4. Show *Gratitude*
Gratitude is a tremendous key to unlock what's in the relationships around you. The people you're choosing to honor have emotional needs, just like you. They need to know that their contributions are making a difference. They need to know that they are creating a legacy that will last beyond them. Communicating your gratefulness and appreciation of them is the quickest way to meet those needs.

If you'll start meeting their needs with your words of gratitude, you'll find them postured to invest in you on a whole new level. When people don't feel appreciated, they tend to clam up and keep their valuable knowledge to themselves. But people who are emotionally filled are generous, bringing the best of their treasure to share with you.

5. Expect the *Benefits*
Even as a young parent, I've noticed that when my need for honor is met, it pulls the best out of me. When my daughter asks me questions and her heart is wide-open to learn from me, I get serious about what I

say. I don't take it lightly. I know that my words are shaping the belief system of another person. It's a big responsibility. Many times I have to analyze my own motives and beliefs to make sure I'm giving the best response.

This is a universal response to honor in all relationships. While dishonor may cause a wounded person to exert control and irrational behavior, honor will often cause them to take a new posture. When you communicate that you value others and want to learn from them, they will rise to the challenge. They'll start weighing their own motivations and thought processes, searching for jewels of wisdom to pull from their own journey. And you will be the benefactor!

P.S. – The Blessing doesn't end with you! While you're learning to access the treasures buried in the people around you, there are others waiting to build on the platform of your success. Are you ready to be generous and allow a new generation to benefit from your experience?

About Harrison

Harrison Wilder is a sought-after communicator based in the Washington, DC area. As an author and speaker, Harrison challenges people with a unique spiritual approach to everyday life. On topics of Leadership, Finances and Generational Relationships, Harrison blends his experience as a pastor with his business background to develop practical solutions for his audience.

Harrison has an Executive Masters of Business Administration from the George Washington University, where he graduated with honors. He is also the Executive Pastor of Capital City Church (www.capcitychurch.com), a thriving multi-cultural church in the heart of Washington, DC.

To learn more about Harrison Wilder, and how you can receive a free copy of his latest e-book, visit: www.HarrisonWilder.com.

CHAPTER 10

MAKING THE WORLD A *MORE* BETTER PLACE:
HOW NON-PROFITS CAN EFFECTIVELY AND ECONOMICALLY TELL THEIR STORY AND FUND THEIR MISSIONS

BY NICK NANTON, ESQ., BOBBY DAVIDOWITZ & JW DICKS, ESQ.

If you think today's ADD Internet users can't sit still long enough to discover the facts about a worthy cause and then do something about it – think again.

In March of 2012, the 30-minute video, "Kony 2012," was posted on YouTube to bring attention to the plight of those in Uganda who were victimized by warlord, Joseph Kony, and his "Lord's Resistance Army" (LRA) guerilla group. The LRA is responsible for numerous atrocities and is accused of abducting over 60,000 children; turning many of them into child soldiers.

In a matter of days, this movie went viral everywhere on the web, racking up over twenty million views in a matter of weeks and raising both awareness and money for this cause. As of September of 2012, the film had over 93 million views on YouTube and almost 17 million views on Vimeo. A poll taken in the days following the video's initial release suggested that over half of young American adults had heard about the "Kony 2012" film.

After this explosive success, much controversy swirled around Invisible Children, Inc., the American charity that produced this film - but the impact of this film was undeniable. The cause is still going strong as we write these words. The non-profit has a big event scheduled in November, and the campaign has already resulted in a resolution by the United States Senate to take action against the LRA. In addition, the campaign has contributed to the decision to send troops by the African Union.

This is a glimpse at how a *30-minute film* can bring a unique power to a message. Not simply a film, however, but a compelling story which was produced, shot, and edited to light a fire in people's hearts and move people to act. Someone decided to do MORE...BETTER.

Isn't it reasonable to think we can do "More Better" for other great causes with this approach?

We think so. As a matter of fact, we've already committed ourselves to doing just that.

MARKETERS FOR GOOD: JACOB'S TURN

The power of film can't be denied, even in its earliest incarnations: D.W. Griffith's early film epic, *Birth of a Nation*, was described as "lightning in a bottle" by then-President Woodrow Wilson in 1915.

Nowadays, however, we mostly think of movies as showcases for fictional superheroes, nonstop chases, and brutal horror movies. This is fine for some, but it just seems that there is a wasted potential when it comes to harnessing the power of a film. Why couldn't such a great medium be used to energize people to do something good? Why couldn't we use movies to change the world?

It turns out we found the answers to those questions – by accident. We discovered how the power of film can be used to achieve great positive outcomes for organizations and causes that desperately need a boost – and this was three years *before* Kony 2012 happened.

It was April of 2009 and Nick was waiting out a layover in a terminal at Midway Airport in Chicago. Nick is always on the go so this wasn't an unusual experience for him. He was sitting next to a guy who was on his laptop – and Nick happened to notice a picture on the display of a boy, about four years old, in a baseball uniform. He couldn't help a smile as he turned to the guy and said, "Cute kid."

Those two words ended up transforming our lives and his.

The guy with the laptop turned out to be a dad from Indiana named Jim Titus – and the picture on his display was of his son, Jacob Titus. His response to Nick's compliment was, "He's an amazing blessing to us." He also added that his son had Down Syndrome.

The conversation continued. Jim told Nick that he worked for UPS; Nick told Jim about our Celebrity Branding Agency and how we managed clients all across the country and helped them achieve high-profile status. He also mentioned his experience in entertainment, producing award-winning albums and television shows.

Jim may have lived in Indiana, as far away from the entertainment industry as you can imagine, but he was still very interested in Nick's background - for a very specific reason.

Because of his son's condition, Jim's family was very involved with the Down Syndrome Support Association of Southern Indiana. The organization was going to hold a silent auction during its annual Buddy Walk event – and Jim wondered if Nick had any "celebrity items" he could contribute. Nick agreed to look into it and they exchanged email addresses. A few weeks later, Nick sent Jim a couple of CDs autographed by country music stars, Rascal Flatts and Bucky Covington, for the auction, and that was that.

Except it wasn't.

Four months later, Jim emailed Nick an article his wife had written about their son which was entitled, "Jacob's Turn." It was a beautifully written article about Jacob's experience playing T-ball that year (which is why Jacob was wearing the baseball uniform in the photo), and it moved both of us to tears.

Jacob's story was amazing – his skills developed over the season and his team almost won the championship; the season ended with the coaches giving Jacob a ball autographed by the local minor league baseball team, The Louisville Bats, as a special prize for his hard work and dedication.

Our agency had been looking for a way to "give back" – and we felt Jacob's story was important. So we wondered how we could help the story go viral to somehow benefit the Down Syndrome Support Association. We finally brainstormed the perfect answer.

That answer? Tell the story in *movie* form – a film that could be placed online and potentially reach millions of people.

Movies are, of course, an expensive proposition, but luckily, we also had access to a circle of expert marketers and entrepreneurs who would probably be willing to help. They ended up pitching in, and with financial backing from all of our new "executive producers," Nick flew into the Titus' home town of Floyds Knobs, Indiana in May of 2010 with a film crew. With the community's help, they recreated Jacob's magical first season playing on a baseball field.

Through interviews with Jacob's family, his coaches, his teammates and other townspeople – and some beautiful cinematography provided by our crew – Jacob's story was fully realized in a seven minute short film entitled "Jacob's Turn." We posted the video online and used our marketing and PR expertise to push the movie not knowing what would happen. It wasn't long before the movie and its message caught fire. The movie was going viral! The movie was so powerful we ended up attracting donations, which helped to pay for some of Jacob's special therapies and classes. We couldn't have been happier with the success of our product and how we were able to help this young boy, however, what came next, none of us expected. Our production team was awarded an Emmy Award for "Jacob's Turn." Wow.

HELPING OTHERS AROUND THE WORLD

The gratifying experience we had with "Jacob's Turn" led us to start our CelebrityFilms® division. CelebrityFilms gave us the opportunity to combine our Emmy Award winning production skills with our PR agency's expertise in producing events, developing multi-million dollar marketing campaigns, and writing Best-Selling books. We were excited about this new venture, but we weren't ready to let go of the charitable good that these kinds of films could do.

As we began making movies for clients, we heard about more great causes through our circle of friends – which we saw as new opportunities to "Market for Good." So, once again, we approached our professional circle to help raise funds – this time on behalf of Esperanza International. Esperanza dedicates itself to helping children and their families in the Dominican Republic escape poverty through initiatives that help fund small businesses, mostly run by women. This initiative not only fosters income, education and health, but also restores self-worth and dignity to those who have lost hope in the process. Esperanza was founded by former Seattle Mariner's catcher, Dave Valle, and his wife Vicky. We are so excited to deliver this amazing movie entitled "Esperanza" (in English this means "Hope") to the organization. They realize, just like we did with "Jacob's Turn," what an amazing tool this movie will be. Rather than Dave having to travel all over the world telling the wonderful story of Esperanza all by himself, he now has a movie that can spread the message on its own. This movie not only has the ability to reach the masses but it allows the organization to tell their story in a real and emotional way - CONSISTENTLY. Consistency is so important. We all know people who are great storytellers, but we also know that many are not. This film allows everyone in the organization from volunteers to employees and donors to tell the story in an amazingly moving way. Just press play!

We are blessed that there is no shortage of opportunities to help. Recently a good friend of ours introduced us to an amazing orphanage in Acapulco, Mexico called *Casa Hogar*. Kids left on the street to fend for themselves have a home there, and more than that, a chance for a future. Kids from *Casa Hogar* actually go to college at 3 times the rate of the average in Mexico! We took a trip there and were not only inspired but saddened. The library had less books than our kid's room. Kids were sleeping on the floor for lack of beds, and their makeshift computer room looked like a computer museum. We actually went to touch what looked to be the first Apple ever made, and the computer fell apart!

So I'm sure you can guess, yes, we wanted to make a movie about *Casa Hogar*; we wanted to expose this cause to new donors and get them the help they need. But how? Well, we brainstormed, and came up with another really cool way to not only raise the money for their film, but to get donors involved even more. "Mission for Good" not only allows donors to be Executive Producers of the film but also has a service project component. Our donors will actually travel with us to *Casa Hogar* and we will stock the library with new books, provide new computers, and paint the rooms. We can't wait! Amazing people coming together for an amazing project; and we get to make a movie about it!

FILMS FOR GOOD: OUR NEW MANDATE

All of these projects made us realize we had to formally establish a special division to produce these kinds of films to benefit worthy organizations that were in immediate need of both publicity as well as donations. "Films for Good" was born.

We realized we also needed a mechanism to raise funds continually for new Non-Profits that need their story on the big screen, so FilmFunding™ became the engine for Films For Good™. FilmFunding™ is the key that allows us to continue to help nonprofits raise the money to produce these important films on their behalf. It's turning out to be an amazing tool to help these causes tell their stories, with no money out of their budget! Once their film is created and marketed, the movie itself will be the key to raising funds for years to come.

We are doing everything possible to make these kinds of film projects feasible for nonprofits because we've seen how important they are to raising their profiles, and even more critically, raising funds. Participating in producing these films becomes a definite win-win, both for the deserving causes involved and for all of us who want to help make the world a better place.

Why do these kinds of narrative movies make such a crucial difference for nonprofit organizations?

First of all, *films create empathy.* One of the reasons they are so effective is that telling a tale causes the audience to put themselves in the shoes of the "hero" of the story – and to feel what that hero feels in his or her struggle to overcome obstacles. When portrayed in one of our films, the cause itself becomes this "hero." We see the odds it must face in trying to do the good deeds it has set out to accomplish – and we end up rooting for it to succeed, just like we'd root for Rocky to win a fight or Iron Man to take out a super-villain threatening the world.

Even though the film is made to benefit a charity, it still works on the same emotional level as a well-made Hollywood film. That's because we leverage the same narrative tools that for instance, Steven Spielberg used to make us care about "E.T." – we've studied them and we know how they work. Of course, it's not hard to create the kind of emotional pull these causes have; when you're exposed to the good work these people do, you can't help but be moved and want to see them succeed.

It's just a matter of finding the most powerful way to portray that work through the structure of a documentary.

Second of all, *films put a face* on an abstract cause. As we all know, it's really easy to say "no" to somebody over an email. When that person shows up at your office or your house asking in person, however, it's a lot harder to turn them down.

Similarly, when you hear an orphanage in Acapulco has inadequate facilities, you might pause for a moment, shrug and say, "Wow, that's a shame" – and go on with your life. However, when you see the faces of those kids in a movie and you actually see the less-than-ideal resources they have to learn with, you can't dismiss the situation quite so blithely. As a matter of fact, it makes most people want to donate *right that second* to improve things for them.

Which brings us to our final point – online films and videos are more popular than ever, and most importantly, *they inspire action.*

We began this chapter by discussing the Kony 2012 video. When it went viral, so did the cause – to millions of people who didn't even know who Kony was. And Invisible Children's donations *tripled* for the fiscal year ending in June of 2012. Even Oprah gave the charity two million dollars.

The statistics back up the power of online video and film. 170 million Americans currently watch online video – that's 53.5% of the population and 70.8% of internet users (up 7.1% from 2011). What's more, according to Internet Retailer, 52% of consumers say that watching product videos makes them more confident in their online purchase decisions.

In other words, an online video or film can convince viewers to *act*. For an online retailer, that action translates into sales; for a nonprofit, that action translates into *donations and support*.

Nonprofits are all about making the world a "more better" place. Our new, Films For Good™ Division along with our FilmFunding™ efforts, are all about making the effort to raise money for those nonprofits "more better" as well.

The power of film is a constant through the last one hundred years or so, in terms of inspiring movements, sharing stories and making a difference. Movies don't have to be just about superheroes and outlandish action. They can easily be about making a real difference.

And we think it's time they were.

We hope this message of what we have learned about the power of film to leverage the story of non-profits and their missions to reach more people, will inspire others to use their gifts to help tell more stories and offer solutions to those in need.

Nick Nanton

An Emmy Award-winning Director and Producer, Nick Nanton, Esq., is known as the Top Agent to Celebrity Experts around the world for his role in developing and marketing business and professional experts, through personal branding, media, marketing and PR. Nick is recognized as the nation's leading expert on personal branding as *Fast Company Magazine's* Expert Blogger on the subject and lectures regularly on the topic at major universities around the world. His book, *Celebrity Branding You®*, while an easy and informative read, has also been used as a textbook at the University level.

The CEO of The Dicks + Nanton Celebrity Branding Agency, an international agency with more than 1500 clients in 26 countries, Nick is an award-winning director, producer and songwriter who has worked on everything from large-scale events to television shows with the likes of Brian Tracy, Jack Canfield (*The Secret*, creator of the *Chicken Soup for the Soul* book series), Michael E. Gerber, Tom Hopkins, Dan Kennedy and many more.

Nick is recognized as one of the top thought-leaders in the business world and has co-authored 23 best-selling books alongside Brian Tracy, Jack Canfield, Dan Kennedy, Dr. Ivan Misner (Founder of BNI), Jay Conrad Levinson (Author of the *Guerilla Marketing* Series), Leigh Steinberg, and many others, including the breakthrough hit, *Celebrity Branding You®*.

Nick has led the marketing and PR campaigns that have driven more than 1000 authors to Best-Seller status. Nick has been seen in *USA Today, The Wall St. Journal, Newsweek, Inc. Magazine, The New York Times, Entrepreneur® Magazine, FastCompany.com.* and has appeared on ABC, NBC, CBS, and FOX television affiliates around the country, as well as CNN, FOX News, CNBC, and MSNBC from coast to coast, speaking on subjects ranging from Branding, Marketing and Law to American Idol.

Nick is a member of the Florida Bar, holds a JD from the University of Florida Levin College of Law, as well as a BSBA in Finance from the University of Florida's Warrington College of Business. Nick is a voting member of The National Academy of Recording Arts & Sciences (NARAS, Home to The GRAMMYs), a member of The National Academy of Television Arts & Sciences (Home to the Emmy Awards), co-founder of the National Academy of Best-Selling Authors, a 13-time Telly Award winner, and spends his spare time working with Young Life, Downtown Credo Orlando, Marketers for Good, and rooting for the Florida Gators with his wife Kristina and their three children, Brock, Bowen and Addison.

Bobby Davidowitz

Bobby Davidowitz is the Senior Producer and part of the Emmy Award-winning production team at CelebrityFilms® in Orlando, FL. His writing, production, and camera skills have been featured on the Universal Sports Network, The Biography Channel, and CNN. He has received 5 Telly awards for his documentary work on Entrepreneur-based films and now focuses on bringing the causes of innovative Non-Profits to life.

Bobby currently heads the FilmsForGood™ initiative at CelebrityFilms®, and as Senior Producer, oversees the search for amazing Non-Profits as well as the production of their films. Bobby is considered a true hybrid in the entertainment industry with over 12 years of experience in music production, video production and screenwriting, as well as on-camera work. As a film producer, Bobby's ability to "see" the story and facilitate the unfolding of that story on camera makes him a standout talent in the movie industry.

Email: Bobby@CelebrityFilms.com
Website: www.CelebrityFilms.com

JW Dicks

JW Dicks, Esq. is America's foremost authority on using personal branding for business development. He has created some of the most successful brand and marketing campaigns for business and professional clients to make them the Credible Celebrity Expert in their field and build multi-million dollar businesses using their recognized status.

JW Dicks has started, bought, built, and sold a large number of businesses over his 39-year career and developed a loyal international following as a business attorney, author, speaker, consultant, and business expert's coach. He not only practices what he preaches by using his strategies to build his own businesses, he also applies those same concepts to help clients grow their business or professional practice the ways he does.

JW has been extensively quoted in such national media as *USA Today, The Wall Street Journal, Newsweek, Inc. Magazine*, Forbes.com, CNBC.Com, and Fortune Small business. His television appearances include ABC, NBC, CBS and FOX affiliate stations around the country. He is the resident branding expert for Fast Company's internationally syndicated blog and is the publisher of Celebrity Expert Insider, a monthly newsletter targeting business and brand building strategies.

JW has written over 22 books, including numerous best sellers, and has been inducted into the National Academy of Best Selling Authors. JW is married to Linda, his wife of 39 years and they have two daughters, two grand-daughters and two Yorkies. JW is a 6th generation Floridian and splits time between his home in Orlando and beach house on the Florida west coast.

CHAPTER 11

HOW TO BECOME A MILLIONAIRE IN PRIVATE PRACTICE

BY P. CHRISTOPHER MUSIC

Note: While this chapter specifically speaks to professionals in private practice (since they are the clientele of the author), the principles contained in this chapter apply equally to any small business owner.

When I graduated from business school with an MBA, I thought I would be able to start and manage my own business. Boy, was I surprised! While I was educated in business administration as a subject, I had no training on how to be an entrepreneur. I began my practice with a hope and a dream, but no real plan or know-how to be successful on my own. I just wanted what every other professional wants: demonstrated competence as a practitioner and the time and money to enjoy my other interests in life.

It's an interesting question:

What would cause a professional—one who is trained in health-care, finance or accounting, sales, or any other technical subject—to leave the safety of being an associate or employee to venture out into starting or buying into a private practice and captaining one's own ship?

Over the years I've heard the reasons: helping people, being able to do what I want, couldn't find anyone who did it the right way, master of my own schedule, and so on. But let's face it, one of the deciding factors to own a private practice is the economic rewards – time and money.

When one makes the decision to engage in that rollercoaster ride called "private practice ownership," he forever abdicates the idea of an ordinary life. It certainly takes courage, skill, and a high tolerance for failure to be successful at this game, but the lifetime rewards can make it all worthwhile—if you play the game to win. For those of us who have endeavored into this fun-filled activity, we learn that it truly is a challenge to run a business; we muddle around with trial and error, tips and tricks from consultants and coaches, or learning about industry "best practices." This is a very expensive and unpredictable way to go about operating your largest and riskiest asset: your practice.

It is unfortunate that we were never taught the realities of running our own business in school. All of that technical training and not a 'lick' of entrepreneurial acumen. Nevertheless, without a command of the functions of business—sales, marketing, organization, public relations, strategic planning, quality control and finance—all of the efforts spent pursuing one's dreams will be spent in vain.

To begin, we must understand that being in business for yourself has three primary responsibilities:

The first responsibility is that of the <u>Technician.</u> This is the implementation of the specific services you provide the public. When one gets started in private practice, the technician is the one who delivers all of the exchangeable value to the public for the money the business makes. These are the skills one attained from all those years in school. As one proceeds through his or her career, the accumulation of many years of continuing education and experience go into creating a professional that can deliver consistent results.

The second responsibility is that of the <u>Executive.</u> Assuming one has the technical competence to deliver a valuable service, then one has to ensure that the business structure is established and maintained to create a stable and expanding organization. The executive has the charge of coordinating the planning, personnel, sales and marketing, finance, public relations, quality control and efficient delivery of the firm's services. This takes a completely different set of skills to the Technician, yet the same amount of training is needed.

The third responsibility is that of the <u>Owner.</u> As an owner, you have the duty to ensure that the business meets the objectives of all of the investors in the enterprise: the establishment and expansion plans, profitability, compliance with legal and regulatory requirements, the attainment of the business' goals and purposes and, finally, its eventual disposition.

In order to become categorically successful in private practice, you have to fulfill each one of these primary responsibilities to professional standards.

To assist you, I have codified *The 10 maxims of the Private Practice Millionaire* (Maxim [mak-sim] – *noun* : an expression of a general truth or principle ; rule of conduct).

I learned these rules through trial and error and a few bloody noses. These principles, applied in private practice with the intention to win, are the best guarantee of success for which I am aware. They are listed as simple attestations as follows:

1. **I will seek to deliver the highest quality service of which I am capable.**
   One of the fundamental rules of a private practice millionaire is that you provide the absolutely highest quality technical results in your professional capacity to the market you serve. This is paramount. You will find that the highest-paid people in any profession are those that get the best technical results. For example, let's take a touring professional golfer. You will notice that the highest paid golfers are those that get the lowest scores. To get the lowest scores, it's done by honing the ideal swing, perfecting the winning tactics, mastering the long and short game, creating an unwavering mental resolve, and achieving enviable consistency. Since these assets are considered valuable in the field of competition and in promotion of the sport, the market creates the opportunity for abundant prize money and endorsement deals.

   The quality of the service comes *before* the money. Just because you're a practitioner does not entitle you to a lucrative career; you cannot expect to earn a good income if you do not provide the highest technical quality service of which you are capable. The way this is done is by continuing education, learning new techniques (or perfecting old ones) and practicing them until the procedure is done perfectly and consistently every single time. Only then can one get past the technical reasons for business failure and into other areas that solve the problems of income, influence and expansion.

2. **I will endeavor to educate the public on the value of my profession's services by becoming a well-respected expert in the field.**
Once you master the technical aspects of your profession, then it is vital that you represent your profession to the public at the highest level of ethics, integrity and competence. No matter the profession, whether dentistry, optometry, fitness, veterinary medicine, law, finance or the arts, you are the representative of your profession to your clients/patients. You are the expert that has the ability, expertise and experience to help that consumer achieve the results they seek. You are the best and the brightest in your field.

The most successful professional is at the top of the field where your profession recognizes you as a leader, master and innovator. Even if the industry hasn't recognized your talents yet, the best way to market yourself to your public is to position yourself as THE expert, THE go-to person for the services you provide. For example, if you are a veterinarian with a small animal practice, then you would do well to educate all of the potential clients in your city about how you have exhausted all of the standard methods and tools of veterinary medicine to find the absolute best technology in pet care for them. Do not assume your potential clients know your technical expertise—they don't. You have to tell them. Use the Internet, direct mail, brochures, referral kits, video and audio media. Write a short consumer guide. You have to show them what the ideal veterinary experience is, and how *you* provide that. Demonstrate your results through getting testimonials – whether written or on video – about how you saved a family pet with your awesome skills. Sooner or later you will be able to leverage the additional recognition from your peers when your competence and influence become more evident.

Don't forget the competitive advantage recognition as an expert will have on your practice. For example, let's take two dentists in a particular market. One has written a technical book or consumer guide and has been recognized by his clients and professional colleagues as being an industry mover and shaker. The other one has not. The first dentist is going to have an easier time bringing in new patients and referrals than one who has not positioned himself as an expert. The one with the greater credibility will always win the battle for new clients/patients and retaining current ones.

3. I will treat my professional practice as an investment, not merely a place to work.
When we go into private practice for ourselves, the basic problem is that we were never taught how to run one, let alone how to own one. As an owner, it is very important that we treat the practice as an investment: an entity into which money and effort has been expended with the expectation of profit.

In my experience, most professionals go into private practice because of the need for independence and the desire to serve their clients/ patients in their own way, which coincidently is the only correct way (smile). Once the business is created, it ends up being a place to go to work every day to practice technical skills rather than becoming an expanding, profit-making machine that has a life of its own. It looks less like a business and more like a job.

Investments create ROI (Return on Investment). The ROI of a private practice is certainly the flexible hours, independence and satisfaction of making your own way. It is also the monetary profit, which for most professions is in the neighborhood of 25-40% – give or take. That is the appropriate rate of return on an investment that has the extraordinary financial risk inherent in such an activity. It amazes me how many owners have profit margins in the single digits or worse! There is a reason J-O-B stands for "Just Over Broke!"

Neglecting to treat your practice as an investment carries the penalty of ending up at the twilight of your career at age 60, 65, or 70 years old without an asset that someone else will find valuable. Buyers of businesses want to invest in profitable assets, not used equipment and a dwindling customer base. Since practices that are profitable and well-managed fetch 50%-100% higher prices than the alternative, it truly pays to learn how to get more ROI out of the activity of owning a private practice.

4. **I will seek to create maximum economic and social value in my practice.**
The value of a business can be summed up in one question: How many lives (clients/patients and employees) have been positively affected by the existence of the entity and by how much?

Maximizing economic value is required so that the practice can survive in our economic and political environment; maximizing social value is the reason the practice has meaning in the lives affected by its existence.

To maximize economic value, several questions need to be answered: Are you going to have just one location, or multiple locations? Will you bring on partners or associates? How many staff are you going to take on? What is the overall purpose and vision of the company? How will the practice be structured legally? How will contracts be handled? What methods will be used to optimize taxes? What will be done to minimize risks and protect company assets? What will be done to overcome regulatory barriers? How will profit be realized? Will the practice survive you or die with you? How big will you get? What products and services will you provide and to whom? And a multitude of other important queries.

The economic value of the practice ultimately answers the question of how much social value is created, provided that the quality of technical services is superb and the staff is considered valuable and integral. The bigger the practice, the more lives can be positively affected by its activity.

5. **I will formulate and implement a written transition plan regardless of when and how I plan to transition or exit the practice in the future.**
Every successful entrepreneur and real estate mogul knows one thing: how to get out of the deal. They work out the exit plan *before* they begin.

If only that was how private practice professionals thought. The concept that there is an end to a professional's career has never crossed his mind with respect to the exit of his practice (not retirement in general). That has been my experience with clients. It seems as though people start a private practice thinking it will go on forever. It might, just not with the founder due to that inconvenient fact that bodies wear out and stop functioning eventually.

Well, it's going to happen. One way or another, you will exit your practice, whether partially or completely. There are seven major ways to exit: dying with your boots on, closing the doors, selling externally, selling internally to successors, selling to a consolidator, selling to employees or giving it away. Of the seven major ways to exit the practice, which one(s) will be utilized and when? What will be done to maximize the value of the practice to a potential successor? How will the disposition of the practice (whether all or part) affect one's household finances and retirement plans?

One has to address these questions, and the sooner the better. The best way to address this area of your professional life is to sit down and actually write-up your exit plan. Write down exactly when you will exit, which strategy you will use, when you will do it, for how much and under what terms (we assist our clients with this process).

Until you know your exit plan, you will not build value in your practice to the degree you should. It's always easier to hit a target that you can see. Remember, you always reserve the right to change your mind.

6. I will perform executive responsibilities in the practice as competently as possible.

Just as you have spent a considerable amount of time learning the technical aspects of your practice, you must become a rock star in the executive functions of the practice. You cannot neglect this area. You need to master marketing, sales, finance, quality control, public relations and leadership skills. This is accomplished by finding a consultant that teaches a proven system. You are looking for a whole system of management that coordinates all of the functions and staff members for expansion– not just tips and tricks. If you want to know what I use, send me an email. Info@Econologics.com.

No matter how you do it, learn and master what works. Becoming a top-flight executive can mean millions to you over a career in private practice. Just ask anyone in the top 5% of income in your industry— they are rock star executives.

7. I will clarify the goals, purposes and values of the practice and align all of my activities and those of my staff to the fulfillment of those aims.

As a leader, you have the responsibility for creating the ultimate manifestation of your practice—what it is and what it will become. Your staff and clients/patients rely on you to lead them toward some known destination: the fulfillment of the purposes of the group.

When I counsel clients on financial planning matters, we start with a statement of the goals, purposes and values then proceed into the necessary actions needed to bring them to fruition. If the owner cannot clearly articulate the goals and mission of the firm, then I know that the rest of the staff cannot possibly know where they are going. This is clearly demonstrated in a lack of teamwork and, interestingly enough, financial mismanagement. This, unfortunately, is a very common state of affairs.

The successful professional is crystal clear in the direction of the firm and can fully communicate it with his staff and clients/patients. Once everyone is on the same page as to the firm's goals and purposes, the rewards of expansion and financial success can be achieved.

8. I will save a significant portion of the annual gross revenue of the practice into household reserves to create stable and secure financial conditions for the practice and its owners.

Professional practices differ from most other businesses due to the fact that the firm's value is derived from the production of the licensed members of the group. This limits the valuation to the 2-4 times earnings range (or 50%-120% of one year's gross income) for a solo or small ensemble practice rather than a much higher multiple found in other types of businesses. Since the firm's profit (or owner's salary and profit) is taken home each year, a substantial portion of that amount must be saved if retirement income is going to be created above any annual income generated by the practice.

The target amount is really one of two options: 30% of total take-home income or 1.5 x your age x $1000, whichever is greater. For age 50, it is the larger amount of 30% of salary and profit or $75,000 (1.5 x 50 x $1000). If you now enjoy $200,000 per year from your practice, then 30% is $60,000. You will need to save $75,000 at a minimum in the current year. It's simple math. If you want to replace that $200,000 annual income from a source that does not take your time and attention, then you will need to have $4 million invested to generate that income at 5% interest per year.

If you do not save the required $4 million, then you will not be able to completely replace your current income. Your retirement pension is all up to you. Don't delude yourself into thinking that the sale of your practice will do the trick (a practice generating $200,000 a year in earnings will sell for no more than $1 million). This amount invested at 5% will pay only $50,000 a year—only about 25% of your current income. The rest is up to you to save while you are in your peak earning years. What lifestyle will you be able to afford in retirement?

9. I will keep the practice solvent and expanding smoothly through correct prediction and management of financial resources.
Money is the lifeblood of a practice. There is no good reason why a professional practice or its owners do not have sufficient cash flow and savings. It comes down to the rock-bottom basics of making sufficient income, practicing thrift, and being prudent in the protection of assets and income sources.

Expenses can be predicted: future taxes, licensing fees, marketing costs, personnel procurement, equipment purchases, etc. The only time a financial emergency occurs is because a predictable expense was not predicted and provisioned. If you are constantly sweating the bills or payroll, then you have to do two things: stop wasting money and start earning it. Just about every professional practice I evaluate is losing at least $100,000 through inefficiency, ineffective marketing and mismanagement. If this is your situation, then get your training as an owner and executive. That is the reason there is not enough money.

10. I will constantly seek to improve proficiency and results in my responsibilities as a private practice owner, executive and professional technician. I will also seek to improve the executive and technical competence of my staff.
True professionals realize the need for constant improvement. That is why I choose to work with those who pursue excellence in their lives. The real pros pursue these three responsibilities to a level of mastery.

However, it is not enough to become proficient by and for yourself. Your staff must also become proficient in technical and executive functions, at a minimum. And this takes an investment of time and money to realize this objective. (Yes, it's expensive. Make your peace with the costs now if you want the prize.)

And what is the prize?

Freedom from your practice. The ability to come and go as you please and on your terms. There comes a point when the owner can simply guide the firm and delegate all of the work to others. However, this cannot happen unless the members of the firm are sufficiently trained to get the job done and can be accountable without constant supervision.

You should be able to leave your practice for a month with no communication at all with the office and return with the income and profit still trending upwards. This *can* be done, and if it's not happening yet, some improvements should be made.

SUMMARY

The *10 Maxims of the Private Practice Millionaire* is the blueprint on how to generate the maximum freedom in terms of time and money for a private practice owner. If these ten simple principles are mastered, there is no limit to what one can accomplish.

After spending 20 years working in the financial planning and private practice areas, I have seen what the application of these principles can do for a professional and his family. It is my hope that you heed this hard-won wisdom to achieve all of the success you desire.

About Christopher

P. Christopher Music, also known as The Financial Prosperity Coach™, is a best-selling author and personal financial expert. He has been seen on NBC, CBS, ABC and FOX affiliates around the country as well as in *Forbes, Newsweek* and various health-care industry publications. Christopher is known for asking the question, "How does one achieve predictable, objectively-measurable and optimal financial conditions as a result of engaging in the financial planning process?" Frustrated with the unpredictable and sometimes disastrous outcomes from inconsistent financial advice, he founded the subject of Econologics®, Results-Based Financial Planning™ to standardize and codify the next evolution in financial planning results for America's households.

Christopher is the Founder of the Econologics Institute, a financial education company providing books and courses on the subject of Econologics to the public as well as acting as a certifying body for the Certified Econologics Specialist™ designation for qualifying financial advisors. He is also President of Econologics Financial Advisors, a Registered Investment Advisor, serving the financial prosperity needs of private practice professionals nationwide through the implementation of the Econologics Road Map™ financial plan.

Christopher is a 20-year veteran of the financial planning profession and the author of industry-specific Financial Success Guides for Private Practice Physical Therapists, Veterinarians, Optometrists and Dentists.

To learn more about P. Christopher Music, The Financial Prosperity Coach™, and how you can gain access to the invaluable information found in found in Econologics, visit: www.Econologics.com or join us on our blog site: www.PrivatePracticeMillionaire.com.

CHAPTER 12

DROP IT LIKE IT'S HOT:
HOW TO LOSE WEIGHT AND KEEP IT OFF
(NO REALLY!)

BY FRANK NASH

As of today, there are thousands of so-called diets/exercise programs on the market. I have researched, tried them with myself and have prescribed to members – a vast majority over the years. The truth is they all WORK…. if you can adhere to them. What they failed to look at is the primary reason that humans need to "diet" to begin with—we have forgotten why we are supposed to eat. We consume haphazardly things that taste good, rather than foods that are nutritionally sound and serve the purpose for which they are intended to be in our bodies—fuel.

Eat anything you want in moderation; everything in moderation is okay. Let's dispense with the myths right now. No one *needs* to eat chocolate cake for dessert, you may want it – but don't confuse need and want. The human body is a perfect machine designed to process natural foods of fruits, vegetables, meats, and grains gathered as man ate to survive. The body needs specific nutrients from food to run at optimum capacity in the same way that your car needs the correct fuel and tire pressure to maintain the factory-stated gas mileage. Human bodies were not prepared for large-scale agriculture and the abundance of over-processed foods that came about as a result. I challenge you to give me solid science that says Twinkies are fuel for the human body – calories they have, but nutrients they don't. There is a difference between calories and nutrients. Can you eat 2000 calories per day of Twinkies and stay alive? Maybe. Will your engine perform at its peak and the exterior remain shiny? I doubt it.

Fact: It doesn't matter what you want to happen in your body, what needs to happen will. Everything that happens in your body originates with humans' ability to survive. (It's our survival mechanism.) It takes approximately 10,000 years for a human gene to alter itself. We are essentially the same as we were 10,000 years ago as humans.

Fact, we were all probably hunters and gatherers and as such, there probably were not many people, if any, with an abundance of body fat. Before you can lose the excess body fat you have acquired, it will be helpful to understand what body fat is and how you gained it.

IF YOU WANT TO LOSE BODY FAT, YOU MUST UNDERSTAND IT FIRST.

What is body fat? Next time you grab your love handle, don't get mad at yourself or the fat; this isn't your body punishing you. Body fat is just "stored energy." Although you probably aren't happy with your body fat, it plays a vital role in survival. When you eat, your body takes what it needs from what you consumed and stores the rest as body fat or stored energy. This survival mechanism allows humans to go for periods – sometimes very long periods – without eating. When your body needs fuel, which it always does, it can get it from only a few sources. If your body is not getting energy from you orally, it will take it from storage (body fat). If not for your body fat, you would have to walk around with a feeding tube, or a bag of food, and eat every couple of minutes, or run the risk of passing out from lack of fuel. If this were the case, we wouldn't last that long as a human race. However, in our abundance society, where we have low nutritional value-high calorie "so called" foods too readily available, we store energy (body fat) at an alarming rate. Remember, if and when you ate 10,000 years ago, which probably was not much…. you might not eat again for quite some time. Your body still has no idea that you can eat McDonalds every three hours! Your body still thinks it's 10,000 years ago!

Also, please understand that the fortified, low value, over-processed foods we regularly consume today were not around 10,000 years ago. We are finding more and more that since they are without any nutritional value, your body can do nothing but store them as body fat, and some of us – based in our genetic make up – may gain double or triple the body fat as others. This completely undermines the whole "a-calorie-is-a-calorie" theory. If you eat 1200 calories a day of nothing but salad, you will get lean, but if you eat 1200 calories of pizza a day; you won't. I beg any nutritionist to argue that. There is no lack of information about the nutrients in our food, so why then do we continue to fuel our bodies with inferior junk?

SOCIAL EATING

It is a fact; we eat for the wrong reasons. Among the reasons we eat: we think it's time, or boredom, depression, wanting " something," thinking we're supposed to, thinking it would be rude to refuse the host, "it's my friend's birthday,"…the reasons seem endless. We eat for almost every reason except the reason humans are supposed to eat – survival.

In the United States, people consume an average of 500 more calories daily then we did just 15 years ago. The increased availability of low-value, highly-processed foods has confused the consumer and led them down a long path of poor food decisions. It is not socially acceptable to eat healthily! If you were to meet a friend for lunch, and decided not to eat, the question would come about, "Is there something wrong?" It might insult a friend that you have chosen not to eat. And if you ordered a small salad and water, you might be ridiculed or asked, "Is that all you're going to eat?" "Are you on a diet?" Or you might be told, "You don't need to lose weight" or "don't lose too much weight" or "It's not healthy to eat such a little amount of food." My opinion on this barrage of comments and questions, from those who surround you, during your quest to eat correctly and your goal to become more lean, comes from *THEY SAY* (the mythical information that's always been around), and a sense of self-insecurity.

Rarely is any gathering of people including business meeting, birthday, date, or party, not accompanied by food or drink, and these so-called foods are usually not of the high nutrient type. I consider myself to be healthy and fit with good eating habits (correct eating habits), yet find myself being ridiculed often for my behaviors.

GENETICS

Your genetics are your genetics, and you can't choose your parents. Some of us are blessed with amazing genetics (professional athletes) and have the ability to consume any and all types of so-called foods and still look like Greek gods; some of us are on the opposite end of the scale where, if we look at a cookie, we gain body fat. This is Fact...no one is created equal.

Understanding where you are is important to your weight loss. Just because your friend can eat pizza, and stay super –lean doesn't mean you can. The reality is, none of these so-called low-value, high-calorie foods were around 10,000 years ago, and your body has no idea what to do with them, and really can't use them because they are absent of any real nutrients. Once consumed, the body cannot make calories magically disappear, it has to do something with them; use them immediately or store them as fat? Think about it. These low-value, over-processed and high-calorie foods, are "poison" to your body. It is not that crazy to think that one would gain body fat by eating them, in fact not gaining from them is unlikely. Start to understand that and that some of us have a greater reaction or irritation from these toxins, and one can quickly surmise how this has reached epidemic proportions in society. Consider the cases in the media about 1000 lb. men. People in extreme weight categories do not necessarily consume ten times the calories of the 200 lb. person, however, their bodies do store ten times more than the average person.

EATING FOR WEIGHT LOSS

I have worked with thousands of individuals and trained over 400,000 sessions over the last ten years. What I know for a fact is that almost all the nutritional information in the fitness world trickles down from two places: bodybuilding and sports performance. I have given tens of thousands of food plans–a vast majority of them based on low-calorie diets requiring 6-8 small meals a day. I was hitting a wall, our members as a whole weren't losing weight. At first, of course, I blamed the members; you're not accurately reporting your calories, you should have lost weight, are you sure it was only one slice of pizza?

Then came an epiphany. Maybe the problem is not the members; maybe it is the plan? I asked myself, "Why am I giving these plans?" The answer was because of the infamous... "They Said."

They said low calorie diets are best. (Really? Eating small amounts of crap that you're already eating is going to help you lose weight?) The food is absent of nutrients, and we aren't really helping you create good, solid habits by allowing clients to consume nutrient-deficient foods even in small quantities. Sugar is a super-addictive force. To achieve diet success you have to cut it off completely. Don't eat a bite of pizza when you know it will lead to wanting the whole pie.

THE MYTHS OF "THEY SAY"

"They say" that people are more apt to stick to diets eating foods they like …eating foods they like? Like is an emotion and you need to get away from eating for emotion, and start getting emotional uplift from losing body fat and feeling confident. Conventional wisdom tells you a calorie is a calorie, but the reality is that 1200 calories of pizza is not the same as 1200 calories of salad. *They* want you to believe this.

"They say" to eat 6-8 small meals a day. NO way. Forcing yourself to eat even when you are not hungry might matter if you are a professional bodybuilder or an athlete but outside of that, it defies logic.

"They say" if I don't eat enough, I'll ruin my metabolism. We've had hundreds of members actually fast up to 36 hours, 3 times a week, and they lose only body fat while actually gaining strength. We recommend a low-calorie, high-nutrient diet of no lower than 800 calories, which is enough to sustain lean muscle. We have seen anorexic people…that's what happens when you aren't getting enough.

"They say" lose no more than 1-2 lbs. a week. Why? If a person weighs 300 lbs. and loses 35 lbs. of body fat in 28 days, that's healthy, not unhealthy as "they say." That person will be healthier and happier.

"They say" I have to eat breakfast, or lunch... why? Because it's breakfast time? "They say" it gives you more energy? Listen, if your goal is weight loss, then eating breakfast when you are not hungry is not a good idea. Then you are eating because of time or because "they said."

Realizing that the bulk of our clients were neither bodybuilders nor athletes; I developed a plan for the everyday weight loss candidate.

OUR METHOD: DISPENSING WITH THE MYTHS

Your first goal must be to understand why you eat poorly. For example, you know why sugar makes you happy while you are eating it; it creates an instant euphoria. Then it's gone like a drug. It is addicting. Think of pizza; you know it's unhealthy and has no nutritional value, but you still eat it because it makes you happy. This is 'Crack' to your body!!!! Ten thousand years ago I doubt if you would ever enjoy food. Humans were probably just happy to have eaten, but when you choose food based on taste or emotional comfort, your body loses every time from not eating in the manner people should to eat. Thank you, modern society, for creating this mess.

Weight loss is not a battle; it is a war. Like war or any serious goal, you don't sort of do it. You must attack it. We attack weight loss hard for the first 28 days (the amount of time it takes to create a habit) We eliminate all low-nutrient-value, processed foods that are super addicting, because like an addict, you cannot have these even in moderation. We break bad habits and create new ones. We help you lose as much body fat in those 28 days as possible – with the norm being between 10-30lbs.

What we found is low calorie plans don't work because people work very hard but don't lose weight fast enough. The pay off is not worth the effort. Would you rather lose 4 lbs. in a month…or 30? Would you rather make $10,000 a month or $70,000?

Losing body fat rapidly and recognizing results becomes more addicting and comforting than any low value, emotional food.

WEIGHT LOSS STRATEGIES

I. Diet Modifications
Recovery shakes are high in value and low in calories. They are a great form of control, as you know exactly what is in them and how much, plus they are easy and take away the difficult decision-making process. In some instances, we might prescribe up to 2-3 shakes a day and possibly a small salad everyday for that 28-day period.

Is it boring? Yes! Eating isn't supposed to be entertainment or excite you — that satisfies an emotion, not hunger. Is it bland? Possibly, but food isn't supposed to be super tasty, that's what got you into trouble to begin with.

Is it enough food to maintain your current weight? No, that's the point. We trick your body into survival mode whereby it's in a caloric deficit and needs more energy than you are providing. Since you are consuming a high nutrient diet and strength training, your body will use up its stored reserve energy (body fat) and make you a leaner.

Will you be hungry? Hungry is a child starving in a third-world country. You will be uncomfortable. Your body is used to a certain amount of energy (calories) and thinks it's the size and shape it is for a reason. Your body does not know you want to lose body fat and trim up, so during this ordeal, all your body knows is its environment is changing. In a caloric-deficit, your body will send a signal—which we perceive as "hunger"—saying, hey, we need more energy to maintain our current state. You don't want to stay at your current state, so you have to ignore the signal and trick your body into survival mode to burn your fat stores. That's where you shrink. Hunger isn't a bad thing; hunger is your friend.

In some instances, I have members try intermittent fasting (periods of time where no food is consumed for anywhere between 16 to 32 hours). We love this because it takes away all options, and works extremely fast. This gets people out of the bad habits of eating for the wrong reasons. After the 28-days, we reprogram clients to eat high nutrients all the time and almost to disregard calories. This will keep you lean.

The question we often hear is, "When I reach my goal weight, can I start eating normally again?" Well, there are two types of normal; socially normal eating (including pizza, fries and soda), and eating for the wrong reasons. Then there's eating like a human is meant to, for nutrient value, not taste, comfort, boredom, social reasons, or time of day. One has gotten you into trouble with body fat, while the other has made you the leaner, happier person.

II. Exercise
Losing weight is your goal, but ultimately changing your body is what we want to achieve.If you dropped 50 lbs. but looked the exact same, only smaller, you might think we failed you!Dieting will get you smaller, but exercise will change your body.

There are many different forms of exercise: Pilates, yoga, running, spinning, martial arts, tennis, rock climbing, aerobics class, etc. We found that the best form of training to aid in fat loss is strength training – a form of weight training that is progressive as you increase strength. One can begin with body weight exercises, and as those become less challenging, add challenges by varying the environment. We achieve this by adding load or making the movement more dynamic.

Strength Training allows you to burn the greatest number of calories in the shortest amount of time. It also stimulates your lean muscles and ensures that you only lose body fat as you shrink, giving you that strong athletic look.

The less fat you have the more you'll see this inner athlete. For optimal Weight loss, I recommend the average fat-loss-client Strength Trains only 3 times a week for 1 hour every other day, because their focus must be shared by their diet, family, and career. Working out and dieting is easy; everything else in your life is stressful and hard, and gets in the way of making you a happier, leaner person.

About Frank

Frank Nash is one of the most in-demand and exciting coaches, writers and speakers in the fitness industry today. He currently spends his time lecturing, teaching, training and writing and is the owner of Frank Nash Training Systems in Worcester, MA.

For the past eleven years, Frank has been committed to achieving excellence in the field of Fitness Training and Performance Enhancement. Frank has helped countless individuals and athletes reach their goals through sound scientific training. Though included in Frank's success are countless high-end collegiate and professional athletes, Frank's true passion lies within weight loss and lifestyle coaching. He calls this "life- changing" training. This is where Frank places a vast majority of his focus. Prior to his efforts in achieving excellence in fitness, Frank, a "personal trainer" by education and passion, created and managed a successful health club. Here he "pioneered" what is today called "small group training" (a form of personal training where the members share the time and cost of the trainer). This propelled Frank into the world of an entrepreneur and spawned his very own health club. Over the last eleven years, Frank's passion for excellence has driven him to help thousands of individuals succeed and to build what has been called: "one of the most successful training clubs" in the nation. His leadership is recognized nationwide, for he currently consults many gyms on the "business of fitness" that stretch from coast to coast.

CHAPTER 13

MRS. GRIN REAPER

BY DR. AVIVA BOXER, OMD

MY HUSBAND, GRIM, IS EXHAUSTED.

Our twins Grit and Gristle miss playing with their Daddy. I am tired of seeing the dark circles under his vacant stare. His hood is ratty and frayed and he hangs onto it even though I have repeatedly tried sneaking it into the Goodwill pile. His scythe is rusty and bent from lack of maintenance. "No time," he says. His hours are long and arduous and there are no vacation or sick days. He has no one to back him up in case of an emergency. It all falls on his shoulders. Suffice to say, we have no life. Work is sucking him dry and I have become a sort of widow to the shadows, if you will.

I am at my wits end. When I talked to my support group, I got the same advice from Mrs. S. Claus, Ms. M. Poppins, Ms. M. Mouse, Ms. H. Lechter, among others. They all said the same thing, "Grin and bear. It is all you can do." Well, my husband didn't fall in love with this gutsy grinning girl for nothing. I just can't sit idly by and see his shoulders droop, his stature shrink and his grace, in the grim world of escorting the dead over the threshold into the afterlife, diminished. You humans need him. I need him. His children need him. He is the caretaker of the space that surrounds your spirit as you pass into the afterlife. And that is no easy task. In his heyday he was a power to be reckoned with. It now is time he is restored to his rightful place. I have decided to take this brewing but unknown problem to you, the public, and plead for your help.

I am pleading with you humans to use your will and volition in the taboo area of death and funerals. Pre-write your eulogy. Make known your legacy. Make your funeral a celebration of your unique imprint on this world, in your own way. It is so easy to be swept away in sorrow and grief that the living, left behind, often misunderstand the will, intention and legacy of the deceased. They design things as they would want them, or as they 'think' their beloved would want it to be.

Instead be proactive in death as you were in life. Amplify your spirit to leap over the threshold and into the hereafter. Do it now, while you have your wits about you, love in your heart, laughs in your belly, thoughts in your head, and blood rushing through your vessels. Do it now, before the shadows are cast over you, before you will meet my husband, Grim, among the silence of the whispers.

Putting it into perspective, one chooses a hairstyle, a cell phone, the color of a car that they like. One chooses a mate, a school, what color to paint the walls, and what food to order off a menu. But little attention is paid to the grand graduation from matter to anti-matter, a shift of paradigm for the soul. Time has come to exercise the will and volition for that moment. Pre-intend, pre-attend, pre-choose, pre-mark death and the passage of your soul. Do not leave it to the choice of another or to chance. The same sacred markers one commemorates at the union on the merging of two souls in a wedding, can and should be for the funeral and passing of the deceased's merging with infinity and everlasting.

Since the dawn of time, humans have misunderstood their bodily transition into the other world. They think they are going to passively float away on some river – so all they need to do is to sleep, give up, surrender, let go and be swept away. You humans think that is "dying in peace." That idea is no farther from the truth than the idea that the sun goes to sleep and surrenders to the moon.

At death, there is a letting go and a grabbing on at the same moment. It is volitional. It is driven by each and every person's will and volition of their spirit, their soul. It is active and alive, and yes, it is the spark before the light goes out. But it takes energy to make that transition. When you humans give up, and at your celebratory moment, become victim to circumstance and the choices and perceptions of another, the weight of passing over the threshold of death falls on my husband's weary shoulders, the great and wonderful Grim Reaper. He must drag you, like dead weight across the threshold. He has to wait for you to wake up, shake yourself off from shock and a startling. He is supposed to be an escort, not a hospital orderly moving a body with dead weight from one gurney to another. Now, when a human uses their own energy and volition at the end of their days, their bodies levitate across the threshold, and are not dragged. In the past many spirits skipped, leaped, ran, even cart-wheeled over the threshold, awake, aware, ready and delighted at what they found. They had shed their worldly weight of the physical and were light and free, their spirit and soul without any encumbrance.

Don't get me wrong. Neither Grim nor myself want pity. My beloved Grim is of a strong constitution. One would have to be to do this kind of job. Humans have become unnecessarily heavy and burdensome in a most magnificent moment. But in days gone by, humans would use their will, desires and preferences right up to and into their passing, and their body would shoot across the threshold into the afterlife.

Now, it is not like that at all. It is common to have a death that is a drugged, draggy, loosey-goosey, dead weight, with a type of giving up passing that has become the norm, not the exception. Humans think that their soul was made ineffective because of illness, accident or murder. They have given the direction of their destiny over to the doctors or the clergy. Not so. Never. Your human spirit and soul is directed by you and you alone, by your will. It never dies. It changes form. It changes in the medium of matter and non-matter, but it never dies. It is time humans stop seeing death as some sort of finish line like that of a relay or a horse race. It is never over; the fat lady never sings the blues; the bucket is never kicked; and another one never bites the dust. Physicists are correct in stating a natural law, that 'energy is neither created nor destroyed, only changed.'

So when my dear husband, The Grim Reaper, escorts…not carries you over the threshold, it is not *his* preference or aversion that decides your course. Only *you* do. But to be awake at the end, volitional up to and through the shift from matter to non-matter is something that you humans can control. My husband's job is sad and hard when he sees you humans floundering, stuck, disoriented, uncertain at such a glorious moment, making it painful, unsettling, uncomfortable and unnecessary.

So I plead with you to wake up to your will. Choose in health how you want your death parting. You have planned christenings, birthday parties, graduations, bar/bat mitzvahs, quincinieras, weddings, baby showers, anniversaries and the like. It is time for humans to bring death, funerals and transition out of the taboo secret, foreboding darkness. Call it yourself: heads or tails, or heads and tails. It doesn't matter. It is both life and death in the moment of passing. Like I said, a letting go and a grasping on…. just like the seasons changing, or the night letting go to the day grasping on. It is a shift. And to be awake, volitional and with your will directing the course, it can feel miraculous and beyond what human words can describe.

Some humans, well-known to you, have put their own fingerprint on the transition of their last moments:

Mr. Harry Houdini, death-defying escape artist, requested that he be interred beside his Mother's grave in Brooklyn and that her letters to him, all of which he had saved, be placed on a pillow beneath his head within the coffin. He also requested that his body was laid to rest in the famous "buried alive" stunt coffin, for which he was known. He liked "the familiarity of the box" and the irony of the symbolism, as well as the chance, however remote, to perform the trick once more to cheat the afterlife.

Mr. W.C. Fields, comedian extraordinaire, requested a funeral with 'no religious service.' Further, though he loathed children, he requested establishment of a "college for orphan white boys and girls; one where no religion of any sort was to be preached." But because he never followed through, none of his wishes materialized.

Crowned Emperor of France, Napoleon Bonaparte, had his head shaved and his hair divided among his friends at his funeral.

Mr. Benjamin Franklin, brilliant statesman, philosopher and inventor, jokingly penned his own epitaph, calling himself 'food for worms.'

The great English novelist, Mr. Charles Dickens emphatically directed that his funeral be inexpensive, unostentatious and strictly private. He demanded of the mourners who attended "to wear no scarf, cloak, black bow, long hatband or other such absurdity."

The well known playwright, Mr. William Shakespeare, with his own particular verse, had chiseled into his tombstone a hex, "Blest be the man that spares these stones, and curst be he that moves my bones." To this day no one has touched his grave.

Mr. Charles Millar, a wealthy Canadian attorney, and known practical joker, left shares in a racetrack to a judge and preacher who were vociferous foes of gambling, but only if they accepted automatic membership into a horse racing club. They accepted. To ministers vehemently opposed to drinking, he left shares of a brewery. They took the gift. To two friends who hated each other he willed his vacation home in Jamaica, which they were to share. And they did. He also held a 'Baby Derby', whereby he bequeathed a fortune to a Toronto woman who "has given birth to the greatest number of children at the expiration of ten years from my death." On accepting the money, the woman had to vow to practice birth control. Though a straight-laced man in life, he turned out to be a devilish joker in death, revealing just how far the living will go for the dead's money.

Mr. Frederick Kiesler, an elder artist, had a younger, not-yet-so-famous artist Robert Rauschenberg attend his funeral dressed in blue jeans. Rauschenberg then rolled in a big truck tire, and with brushes and jars of shiny colors, he brushed on color in spokes or rays around the flank of the tire. When he was done, the young Raushenberg gathered up his tools and departed, leaving a most beautiful wreath of colors as a gift to the imagination and memory of his mentor, the deceased.

So I ask you humans to craft your own final moments of flesh your way, with your legacy, and with your own will and intent.

I can offer you humans a few questions to ask yourself in the crafting of your funeral so that you exercise your will, while you are well, and distanced from illness, weakness and death.

To get you started, you can customize your last earthy punctuation mark on the story of your life. A great eulogy makes a memorable funeral. One way to make sure your legacy is not left to chance and misinterpretation is to write a self pre-written eulogy. If at birth your first word was a gasp and a cry, let your last words be a cry and a sigh, because you eked out every drop of living, and you are satisfied about the life you have lived fully.

The ghostwriters at WordsmithEulogies.com recommend you answer these questions before you attempt to write your own or anyone else's eulogy:

1. Whose voice do you want to speak?

    a. Your own experience of the departed.

    b. The departed.

    c. The community's experience of the departed.

2. What do you want the other mourners to feel at the end of your eulogy?

    a. Grateful.

    b. Communion and understanding.

    c. Surprised and delighted.

    d. It has been a healing salve.

    e. It has been done with dignity and class.

    f. They have learned something new.

    g. It was one last unique experience and one that the departed would have liked.

    h. It supported and restated the point of view and the preferences of the departed.

    i. The departed left a last taste of him/herself for all of us.

    j. We finally get to know the real him/her.

    k. We now know his/her unfinished projects, ideas and intentions.

    l. The family name, customs and ritual have been honored.

3. What type of griever are you?

    a. A Souler: letting the clergy lead, reconciling the 7 deadly sins with the 7 heavenly virtues.

    b. A Weeper: melancholy, reminiscing about memories, defining the void left, discharging sorrow, making way for healing.

    c. A Laugher: Letting laughter and humor be the healing medicine that unites and bonds the mourners.

d. Ripley RIP, the strange, rare and peculiar: Making known the unusual and precious treasures of the deceased, recognizing that the combination of the mix of qualities in the deceased will likely not be seen again.

4. How involved and interactive do you want the attending mourners? Knowing how one wants others to feel at their own funeral can be translated through words in a eulogy, much like how a singer leads the ears and hearts of her audience with how she feels the story, when she sets lyrics to melody. With the end in mind, the architecture becomes a creative endeavor. WordsmithEulogies.com has various architectural structures for various eulogies and can be a great assist in helping lift the will to the heavens in writing a eulogy.

So, as the alpha meets the omega, and with the end meeting the beginning, let me bring your voice back to my girlfriends in my support group who advised me to "Grin and Bear." Let me tell them that they underestimated the human heart, mind and soul. Prove to them that you want to amplify the sound of your soul as the hereafter calls your name. And just like you did as a baby entering the earthly plane, gasping and crying, kicking and screaming, do the same in death, loudly announcing your presence, your way, …through the birth canal of life into the brightness of the afterlife.

About Aviva

Dr. Aviva Boxer is a speaker, writer, author and natural health-care practitioner. Considered a "double agent" in the medical world for over 35 years, because she has worked both on the conventional pharmaceutical side and the alternative sides of medical treatment. She is well-known for being a Doctor of Oriental Medicine, Herbalist, Acupuncturist, Homeopathic Doctor, and Naturopath. Upon observing individuals who in life were intensely involved in prevention and actively involved in healthful activities and choices in vitality, then they suddenly changed at death's door. They would become passive and vulnerable, delegating their will and their defining moment of personal destiny to another as they passed into the afterlife. Dr. Boxer decided to make it her mission to inspire individuals to amplify their will and preference at and through death, just as they had done in life. She is a writer for: www.WordsmithEulogies.com, "Ghostwriter for the dead and those who need a voice."

WordsmithEulogies is to Funerals what
Houdini was to magical escapes,
Tesla was to electricity and
Hawkings is to black holes.

You grieve and heal while Wordsmith Eulogies secretly writes as if they are the best of you, so that you can avoid the wrenching humiliation, embarrassment and disappointment of your family and friends and mostly of the dearly departed in you, from the afterlife.

She can be contacted at:
WordsmithEulogies.com
(530) 2-Eulogy

Wordsmith Eulogies
PO Box 5301
Playa del Rey, CA 90293

CHAPTER 14

ACHIEVING THE 'IMPOSSIBLE'

BY NICOLA GRACE

"But I haven't done what I came here to do yet. I don't want to die." Words I hope you never hear crying out from deep within your heart, as they did for me.

It was my darkest hour. I was only 29 and hadn't had my first Big Love or lived my dream. My first book tour had just ended and I was sitting up in bed feeling exhausted, bruised, bereft of life as it turned out, facing a six-month termination date. I had Leukaemia. The light had gone out in my mind and it was dark. I didn't know what to do, what to think or where to turn. It was so dark, and it was about to get darker.

I imagined telling my family I was going to die and within seconds my chest tightened, I could barely breathe and I began to sob hard. At the most intense point of sobbing, a small girl's voice came up from within my aching heart and cried out, "But I haven't done what I came here to do yet. I don't want to die." As you can imagine, I lost the plot. I thought I had reached bottom only to find I had further to sink. The Hoover damn of despair let loose in my body until I was so depleted I simply didn't have the energy to cry any more.

Faint as the voice that spoke next was, yet powerful in her message, that little girl called out, "I want to live." A light came on in my mind as I clamoured for some glimmer of hope that I might find a way to live so that little girl could fulfil what she had come here to do. I didn't know what that was, but I knew it was something, I hadn't done it yet, but I had to find it.

What happened next was a series of spiritual experiences – culminating in a profound awakening that took me right into my subconscious mind and plucked out the cause of the cancer at the consciousness level. While I then set about to work a rigorous program of emotional and physical restoration, I knew the big C had moved out of my consciousness. Or so I thought.

Fast forward twelve years to mid 2005, and I'm sitting in the Surgeon General's office being told I needed to have much of the lower part of my left leg cut off to give me only a thirty percent chance of survival past three years. I was in the final stages of Melanoma. In a state of disbelief I returned home and slunk into bed pulling the duvet covers over my head. Steering at the wall I asked the questions why me and why me again? I didn't drink. I didn't smoke. I didn't take drugs. I've lived a relatively healthy lifestyle, helped people where I could, other's who lived debauched lives were healthy – darn it all, I'm a vegetarian! Why me and why me again, it's not fair, "I might as well eat, drink and be merry for tomorrow I could die" I winged to God. On my 'pity pot' I cried out. "If my recovery from this is dependant on going back to eating only raw food, taking buckets of supplements and living a stress-free lifestyle, I'm not going to make it."

I had become that stressed out running a small organic spa and preparing it for franchising, a lifestyle change was out of the question. This time my recovery would have to be dependent on me changing my cancer consciousness, because I wasn't ready to depart and I couldn't see how I could integrate lifestyle changes and hold on to my business at the same time.

A few months later, I was one of two women in a room of men – many of whom had built multi-million dollar businesses. The billon dollar change agent industry they were part of was facing an irreversible and disastrous event that would put many of their businesses under. A petite, powerful and power-dressed woman, one of the highest paid lawyers in the nation, was delivering a doomsday scenario admitting nothing was going to stop the Governments of New Zealand (my home country) and Australia amalgamating their health regulators to form a pharmaceutical dominant corporate entity to regulate natural health products. The managing director of this corporation would have autocratic power to change and make regulations, dramatically departing from New Zealand's current regulatory model. We all knew the corporate regulator would leave the New Zealand natural health industry in tatters.

Rather than feel defeated, I felt a power surge within me. A vision of the certain outcome that we could overturn this destructive course of action flashed before my eyes. I took a look around the room and saw these bright men looking beaten down. For seven years they had worked hard to prevent this day. Here it was, the eleventh hour, up against the wall and out of solutions. I saw one man slouching into his chair, shoulders hunched over, hands over his family treasures, conquered before the event had even taken place.

I'm afraid what I did next was not lady like, so apologies in advance to the more sensitive among you. You see I stood up in my gym gear and said to this high-paid designer label lawyer "Are you saying roll over and get 'f'd now because you're going to get 'f'd later? I can't accept that. I believe we can win this thing."

I think I had just stood up and begun to do the very thing I came here to do.

Shaking in my shoes after I realized the enormity of what I had done, I stood there strong and certain because I had a vision and I had a plan. A MASTER PLAN as it turned out. I had overcome the impossible odds of a death sentence once, and was on the way to doing it again. I had the naïveté that I could lead this billion-dollar industry to victory.

The long and short of it was that I implemented a strategy, and worked alongside several other organizations, health-freedom-friendly politicians and consumers who all played their part, stopped the Government's pet Bill from becoming legislation and made history. You see no one had ever defeated an incumbent Government Bill in peacetime and no one has done it since me.

Why not? Why was I able to achieve in just six months something that an entire billion-dollar industry had failed to do in seven years? What was the magic formula? And most importantly to you - is it duplicatable and universally applicable? Can you use this formula and apply it to your mission or business to make a difference or change the world even? Well, you have my baby brother all of six feet to thank, because the answer is yes, my plan is duplicatable in both the profit and not-for-profit arenas.

My brother congratulated me on my success and said, "That's great Nic, now all you have to do is take that success and apply it to your own business." That got me thinking. I began to dissect the steps I took and examine why they had been successful when others had failed. I went on to work with a strategy consultant to Fortune 500 companies and I came up with ten duplicatable steps that I now mentor entrepreneurs through – called my Ten Step M.A.S.T.E.R P.L.A.N. – that uses "Strategy With Spirit" and the "Undefeatable Laws of Nature" to overcome big obstacles and achieve even bigger results.

The first step is to *Magnetize Your Mission Accomplished.* Creating magnetism that will bring to you the people, events, resources and things needed to accomplish your mission, is foundational to why you will succeed without suffering from burn-out. This step was not only foundational to my success, ultimately it was part of how I beat cancer the second time around. Without this "magnetic foundation" you may or may not reach your desired destination and you'll create unnecessary 'efforting.'

You begin to create magnetism by getting clear on your life purpose, your Soul's chosen primary expression modes and your *raison d'être* (your personal mission). Once defined, you then align them with the Undefeatable Laws of Nature as you write your mission strategy. Ok, so I'm forewarning you, I'm getting really spiritual with you. I realise this might seem way out there for some, but my Strategy With Spirit aligned to the Undefeatable Laws of Nature, was critical to why I achieved in six months something an entire industry failed to do in seven years, so bare with me on this.

I used all the knowledge and power available to me as a whole spiritual being living a human existence. Instead of using only your human body and a small percentage of your brain, why not use all the resources that are available to you? It's like blundering through the world blind, deaf and dumb, trying to solve the world's problems when we don't understand and use the very laws that govern our physical existence. Yet when we operate with these laws and our Soul's Mission, we not only create magnetism we have Soul Power to achieve greatness.

Millions of people use the Law of Attraction to manifest a great car, hot babe or dude, soul mate, dream home, etc. Why not use that Law and other Laws of Nature to make a difference, change the world and make it a place we all feel proud to live in? I believe it's time to fire up on all cylinders of our existence. The world and the people suffering in it could sure use some Soul Power. I think we've had enough of abusive power. What do you say?

So let's *magnetize your mission accomplished.*

Start by defining your purpose, your soul's primary expression modalities and your reason for being. Living true to your Soul's mission gives you personal magnetism, automatic credibility and natural influencing powers because you are congruent with your Soul. When you meet someone who is congruent, you see they radiate a personal power and magnetism. We are attracted to them much more than those who talk the talk but don't walk the walk right?

The next phase is to align your purpose with your actual mission strategy. If the role you play within your mission is doing something other than what you were born for, you'll have to manufacture the drive it takes to reach your successful outcome, and that can be exhausting. Living on purpose in your authentic expression gives you natural and renewable drive, passion and enthusiasm. In my mission I never stepped outside my purpose and Soul's four primary modes of expression – writing, educating, speaking and travelling. That's all I did, everything else got delegated. I never got tired, I never got sick, in fact it began my process of restoration to perfect health.

You have probably heard countless stories of people who have had tragedies, gone bankrupt, got sick and said it was the best thing that happened to them, like me. This is because we're forced to realign to what is important and connect with our real reason for being here. Our life does have a blueprint for our success and highest outcomes. Yes, I'm getting out there. But come on out here with me, the water is fine. Imagine, if you will, you are walking down the straight narrow path of your life blueprint – this is the path that has been mapped out for you that gives you the greatest expansion, evolution, joy, happiness, abundance and success. You wander off down a cul-de-sac only to have to come back to that blueprint path because you came to a dead end. Has that ever happened to you or someone you know?

Imagine with me once again, you walk down another side road which is bumpy, full of prickly bushes, ditches, swamps and unexploded mines. You relentlessly have to deal with one obstacle, disaster or tragedy after another – until you realize you're on the wrong path and you're getting nowhere. Now you have to find your way back to the right path. Life circumstances always work to keep pulling you back on track to your life blueprint. The more you ignore those pulls, the bigger the impending event awaits you somewhere sometime in your life.

Why not stay on your life blueprint path and stick to it? How much more speed do you think you'd pick up toward your desired destination if you stopped wandering off on distracting paths? Knowing what track you should be on and sticking to it builds magnetism and momentum, because you're not wandering off.

The third phase to magnetize your mission strategy is to make sure you are aligned with the Undefeatable Laws of Nature. These are the Laws or principles in physics that govern our physical universe. If your mission statement, your plan and strategy go against The Law of Expansion, The Law of Growth, The Law of Periodicity, The Law of One, you will struggle and you won't have the magnetism of the Universe working with you.

The Law of Expansion, in particular, was why I was able to defeat an opposition bigger than me, more qualified than me, richer than me and more powerful than me (or so they would think). I knew the Law of Expansion always breaks up contraction, constriction and restriction– eventually. As a humanity, we are here to expand and evolve. Any mission that seeks to curtail that expansion will ultimately fail in the long run. It is only a matter of time, and that is the Law of Periodicity (Everything has periods of birth, growth, fruition and decline). I used the Law of Periodicity to make opposing forces smaller than me and bring them into decline faster. The team I worked with also handed the opposition a solution so they could start a positive cycle of birth, growth etc., so we didn't collect 'bad karma' for bringing the opposition into decline.

Aligning with the Law of One is also an important key to overcoming seemingly unsurmountable opposition and achieving the impossible. I never saw the so-called opposition as a separate entity from me. In the embodiment of the Law of One, at the sub-atomic level where all cells in our body and all atoms in nature are at one with this Universal Creative Intelligence, there is no separation. Therefore, there can be nothing that opposes me or my plans if they are aligned to the Universal Laws. They are undefeatable. When we align with them we become undefeatable. Working Strategy With Spirit and the Undefeatable Laws of Nature you have the ultimate leverage system to achieving 'more' and 'better' because you're using more of your entire potential in a better, more efficient way.

You are far greater than you think you are. You are capable of so much more than you achieve today. You have within you Infinite Creative Intelligence that you can work with to achieve your Grand Mission and Most Magnificent Vision for humanity. Like me, you have something you came here to do - a mission - and you have a compelling reason to do it.

You see during my cancer recovery I discovered I had a pretty big death wish. I didn't want to live in this world because there was too much pain and suffering. I have a compelling reason to be about my mission to make this world a better place, because I'll start checking out if I don't. My life quite literally depends upon me doing what I'm here to do. And the truth is at some level –so does your life depend upon you doing what you're here to do. When you find the "I have to do this" in you, you will summon up mighty forces seen and unseen that clamour forward to help you accomplish your mission, as those forces did and do, for me.

What have I come here to do?

What's my mission?

I help people who want to make the world a better place achieve their mission using Strategy With Spirit and the Undefeatable Laws of Nature, so they can experience the satisfaction of knowing they have done what they came here to do, without EVER having to feel the pain of a life unfulfilled.

About Nicola

Recently honored with an award for implementing a strategy that saved a billion dollar industry from ruin and make history, **Nicola Grace** "The Mission Mentor," teaches difference makers and change agents how to create winning mission strategies using The Undefeatable Laws of Nature, to achieve big results without getting stuck in relentless obstacles.

Author of *The Mission Mentor's Handbook for Change Agents*, Nicola is an educator, public speaker and visionary with twenty years experience speaking to audiences globally. Her expert insights appear in the ground-breaking book: *Ready Aim Captivate - Put Magic in Your Message and a Fortune In Your Future,* **along with other world leading visionaries Deepak Chopra and Jim Stovall.**

For over twenty years, Nicola has captivated her audiences as an inspirational speaker, visionary, educator and transformation leader. She made history with her "Ten Step Master Plan" to achieve her mission in 2006. She has defeated two different types of cancers with short expiry dates and gone on to teach her Master Plan to individuals, organizations and entrepreneurs all to successful results. She is the undisputed expert on how to achieve your mission, even when you face insurmountable odds.

While many speakers in her field are motivational and transactional, Nicola Grace is transformational. Nicola is also an active humanitarian with a grand vision for the elevation of ALL of humanity that she would like to share with you.

To learn more about Nicola Grace, The Mission Mentor plus how you can receive free video training on her "Ten Step Master Plan" that combines Strategy With Spirit and the Undefeatable Laws of Nature to **make your mission undefeatable; help you easily turn Big obstacles into Big results** and **achieve your vision in super speedy time visit:** www.TenStepMasterPlan.com

CHAPTER 15

GETTING TO MORE AND BETTER

BY NATALIA J. PEART, PHD

Several decades ago, I began my career as a Clinical Psychologist working with clients in both private practice and in non-profit organizations. I eventually transitioned my career to business consulting and executive coaching. One of the biggest changes I have seen over time is how much people must now take charge of their own career and well-being. Gone are the days of employers taking care of employees until retirement. Now, whether you work for a large corporation, small business, or are self-employed, we all must see ourselves as being entrepreneurs over our own lives. Entrepreneurs see themselves as the architects of their destiny and we must all adopt that paradigm and mindset.

What I've also noticed is that for many, while they want professional success, that is not enough. More and more, the common yearning is that clients want to merge both personal and professional success so that their daily lives are a manifestation of who they truly are. They want to get up each day, and regardless of how busy their lives might be, they want to care deeply about their work. They are looking for more than just success—they are looking to make a significant contribution and leave a legacy in a way that matters to them. They are yearning to create lives of meaning and to live to full capacity. This is "More." This is "Better."

We all know that life has a way of leading us in many directions. What you planned to do for a career while in college may be quite different than what you are doing today, and it may be even something different in the next five to ten years. You also know that sometimes you sought out the change, and sometimes the change found you.

Most people would agree that they want a life with more personal and business success and fulfillment. However, to get from where you are to where you want to be requires change, and most people have a love-hate relationship with change that prevents them from moving forward. They want the result of the more fulfilling life or better career path, but they allow fear and worry of the unknown to stifle their journey. If you want to live more and live better, that requires you to examine the path you are on to make adjustments and midcourse corrections.

One scenario that I often see is the client who feels they have reached or are reaching the pinnacle of their current career. Even though the outside world sees their level of success and they also can see their own level of success, it's not enough. They want to be able to correct themselves midcourse, but they don't know how. They have built a successful career, but along with that came a large mortgage, car payments, college tuition, and other significant life obligations. Instead, they become paralyzed by the thought of how to even begin to think about untangling themselves in a way that allows them to take their life to that place of more and better. They become stuck.

MAKING WAVES

The above scenario is just one way in which some might think about and respond to a new life direction. In my work I have noticed there are three distinct groups of people when it comes to how we process change in our lives.

- **Wave Creators** not only embrace change, but they seek out opportunities to make the necessary course corrections to follow their own path or adapt very quickly to sudden or unexpected situations. They move confidently toward what is ahead despite the uncertainties. In other words, they "lean" into it. They are not necessarily interested in getting bogged down in details at the outset; rather, they are excited by the very idea of big and innovative changes.

- **Wave Riders** are not necessarily leading the changes, but they can and will, with some guidance, adapt to their circumstances and ride it to wherever they must go. Even though they might initially be overwhelmed by the thought of change, these are individuals who can adapt rather than be stymied by the change. While it may take this group some time to warm up to the new idea, with some reflection, they can get on board as long as it is logical and they can see visible results of their efforts soon.

- **Wave Resistors** instinctively want to hang back on the shore and wait until it is over. The will often say "But this is the way we've always done it in the past." In other words, they are unwilling to lose sight of the shore. It doesn't matter if hanging out on the shore is to their own detriment, they will do it as they've always known it or as they've always seen it. Because they are so gripped by what feels comfortable and familiar to them, they are not going anywhere or doing anything differently.

Most people are either Wave Riders or Wave Resistors and are therefore motivated by the avoidance of pain as opposed to the goal they want. This is critical to understand, because while most of you reading this right now can identify that you want More and Better in your life, the truth is, you are likely to be more motivated to avoid the uncertainty that change will bring to your life, than the potential benefits of the changes you want. So instead, for many, the pain has to get completely intolerable before they will take action. They need for their circumstances to completely fall apart around them before they will act. They choose not to read the handwriting on the wall when it appears since it will often take them to a place they are not ready to go. Wave Creators, however, can listen to and hear the still small voice within that leads them to new shores before it becomes the loud roar they can no longer ignore.

When you stop to think about it, when we examine our lives, we are most defined by those moments when we must take a discontinuous turn from what we have known to be normal. The straight and narrow course of our life is not what defines us. What defines us are moments that call on us to dig a bit deeper within ourselves in order for us to live higher, lead higher, and lift others higher.

THE MOST IMPORTANT DECISION YOU WILL MAKE

So, what separates those who successfully dig deeper and handle change from those who do not? Based on my years of work with both clients and organizations, it begins with one key decision: **Perspective**. This is critical because your thoughts create your reality. Those who are successful focus on what they can gain from the changes, whereas those who are not successful focus on what they are losing. I have also observed five habits that characterize those who gain the right perspective and use opportunities for change to their benefit.

THE FIVE HABITS OF SUCCESSFUL
AND FULFILLED PEOPLE

1. Your Relationship to Change

- To successfully embrace change you need to consciously be aware of your own relationship to change so you know how you can best prepare and respond to it. Where do you fall on the spectrum of Wave Creators to Wave Resistors? Do you embrace the thought of change or do you want to avoid change at all cost? Or, are you somewhere in between? To transition through change successfully, your perspective must be one that embraces change as a necessary and positive part of your growth.

2. Acquire Perfect Eyesight

- You must have perfect eyesight or, to put it another way, you must focus relentlessly on where you are going. Those that are successful know that emotions such as fear are a natural part of the process, but they consciously hold the vision of what they are gaining in their minds eye with such detail and clarity that this positive vision of the end result is more vivid than any fears associated with the change. Developing the habit of "seeing the invisible" will move you forward to 'more and better.'

3. Behave Your Way to Change

- Successful people know that you must behave your way into what you want. They know they must take action that is born out of carefully crafted, realistic and manageable steps to get to the desired goal. They don't wait until they feel excited about the change before aligning their behavior to be consistent with the change. Instead, they just do it. They know that their forward movements and the success and positive reinforcement that come from those actions will in turn help build their feelings of excitement regarding change.

4. Follow Positive Role Models of Success

- Successful people seek out positive role models of what they are trying to achieve. You can't be what you can't see, so proper role models provide a reliable source of constant inspiration and encouragement along the journey.

5. Surround Yourself with Optimistic People

- Successful people know they should surround themselves with others who can help them navigate the change. They will focus on others who are also approaching change with optimism and confidence so they can create the right support system for themselves. These supporters can also keep them on task and accountable for their goals.

PUTTING IT ALL TOGETHER

So what does this all mean for you? For most, it means that in order to successfully get to 'More and Better,' you should not approach life transitions as though you need to make a drastic step all at once, like walking off a cliff. Instead, what you should imagine is walking gracefully and carefully up a ramp. In other words, taking small steps upward. When you think of it as taking a leap and jumping off the proverbial cliff, it can be very frightening and paralyzing. If for example, you are considering a career change, thoughts will race through your mind such as, "How am I supposed to walk away from my job? What will I do for income?" Remember that making big changes doesn't have to happen overnight. It does not need to happen in one day, one week, or one month. The question to consider is, "How do I wisely and deliberately leverage my strengths, talents and my current situation to get to my ultimate destination?"

Some people definitely know the new direction they will be pursuing while others don't know exactly what they want to do, but know they want to do something different. If you don't have any idea where you want to go, you should start with determining your natural abilities and what motivates you. When we build a successful career it is usually based on skills that we have practiced over the years. That is not always the same as the things we are most motivated to do or the most passionate about. Our careers are many times based on the things in which we have built strong competencies, but a strong competency doesn't always equate to what we are most passionate about, what we are the most motivated to do, and what gives our lives purpose. That's why most people feel successful, but unfulfilled. We spend our lives climbing the ladder, gaining the skills, and building competency in our job, but somewhere we lose sight of the activities that we were engaged in when we were younger; the ones that we would do for hours on end because we enjoyed it and it was our natural gift–the things that bring out the real passion within us. What are you most motivated by, the most passionate about, and what brings purpose to your life?

While I am sure you can fondly recall what motivated you and what you loved to do when you we were "in the zone", many of us have a set of limiting beliefs that keep us stuck. You might say things like, "I can't make money at what I enjoy" or "It's too late for me to turn back now." These kinds of beliefs will limit our perception of what is possible in our lives. What are the beliefs that are limiting you?

LISA'S STORY

One of my clients, Lisa, was a very successful marketing executive. She came to me at the point where she didn't know how to figure out what she was going to do next. What she did know was that she had a great family life, what should have been the perfect job based on what she loved to do, and in many ways the proverbial charmed life. When I started working with her, she was confused by the paradoxes that she felt were recurring in her life. She was noticing that every time she got a promotion, accolade or something that should have been a cause for celebration, she was left feeling even emptier, more unfulfilled, and more frustrated. These markers of success were only good for a little while, but then she was unhappy again. What I started to notice was that she was sabotaging herself and it was getting harder and harder for her to perform at the level to which she had grown accustomed.

What she didn't realize was that these were the first signs that it was time to re-examine her goals. As I mentioned earlier, for most of us, the initial signs of needing to shift start out as very subtle. The initial signs were hinting to her the foundation on which she based her life was beginning to weaken. Then like many people, an overall unhappiness began to cloud her life. When I began coaching her, I helped her better define who she really was. What we discovered was that Lisa is an entrepreneur at heart. It didn't matter how many promotions or accolades she received from her employer, what ultimately mattered to her was to have something she created that came from her personal drive and determination. Anything else that she was doing, as wonderful as it was, belonged to someone else. When she came to that realization, she determined she wanted to start her own marketing agency.

She didn't immediately walk away from her current career, but she did eventually find a business partner that shared her entrepreneurial passion and who had complimentary skills and strengths, enabling them to become co-founders of their new marketing agency. It allowed Lisa the entrepreneurial opportunity that she wanted, while at the same time allowing her to stay in the business space where she had honed her skills originally.

So, as you can see, 'more and better' doesn't have to be a radical departure from where you are currently, it may simply be a matter of degree. The challenge is to allow yourself the courage it takes not to be stymied by self-doubt, fear, and limiting beliefs. The bottom line is this: if you want to live 'more and better', you must be willing to see yourself as the architect of your own life and the changes you need to make. It is only then that you can experience the rare satisfaction of not only obtaining the success you are looking for, but also the opportunity to make the contribution you deeply desire.

About Natalia

Natalia is an expert in helping clients achieve business and personal success. She has more than 20 years experience as a clinical psychologist, a leadership and performance consultant for national organizations where she worked with senior level executives and management teams to understand strategic and management issues, an executive coach, and as a CEO of a nonprofit organization.

With her varied career experiences, she has become adept at helping individuals and organizations affect change by taking new strategic directions or helping clients position themselves for success.

Natalia holds a Bachelor of Arts degree in Psychology with Honors from Brown University and a Ph.D. in Community/Clinical Psychology from the University of Maryland. She completed her clinical internship at Harvard Medical School/Boston Children's Hospital.

Natalia has been a member of the Board of Directors of the Federal Reserve Bank of Kansas City Omaha Branch, and the University of Nebraska's Medical Center Board of Counselors. She was named a Woman of Distinction by the Midlands Business Journal.

Aside from her coaching and consulting business, she is a frequent keynote, seminar and workshop presenter.

To learn more about Dr. Natalia Peart visit: www.nataliapeart.com

CHAPTER 16

SWITCHING ON MIKE'S FRONTAL LOBE:
RAISING A GMAT SCORE TO 710
& MAKING A QUANTUM LEAP TO
A "MORE BETTER" DESTINY

BY HELENA REILLY, MA

"The major factor that distinguishes human beings from all other species is our large frontal lobe, and the ratio of that frontal lobe to the rest of the brain. The frontal lobe is an area of the brain that enables us to focus attention and to concentrate. It's central to decision-making and to holding a firm intention. It enables us to draw information from our environment and our storehouse of memories, process it, and make decisions or choices different from the decisions and choices we've made in the past."
~ From the book "What the Bleep Do we Know!?"
William Arntz, Betsy Chasse, Mark Vicente

We all possess the capability to transform the repetitive behaviors that no longer serve us. The innate capacity for change hidden within our physiology is extraordinary. The story that I am about to tell is the unfolding of one young man's potential for growth and change. This illustrates that we all have pure potential if we will just awaken to the significance of switching on the frontal lobe. Like switching on a light, this one act will open our life to unknown possibilities. The frontal lobe is the gateway to an enhanced (More-Better) result.

157

August 1, 2010: The phone rings. It is my son Mike calling me in frustration, "I keep getting a 500 or 550 on my practice GMAT. I've decided that if I'm not smart enough to do this, it is okay with me." The GMAT is the more advanced version of the SAT required for entrance to graduate school in finance and business. Many are stopped at the gate of entrance to the elite business programs by this single number alone. Mike had begun studying for the GMAT in the summer after his freshman year of college. He also had set the summer of his sophomore year aside to prepare for the GMAT while doing an internship in Finance.

I will always remember that day and those powerful words from my son Mike …"not smart enough." As a mother and someone with a clinical psychology background, I realized how influential and extensive the effects of our conscious or unconscious thoughts can be on one's outcome. These words of Mike surprised me. Since birth, Mike had always been a go-getter –brilliant, inquisitive and always ready to take on the next challenge. From the age of eight, he chose to be in the ice hockey rink as a goaltender. Now Mike was going into his junior year of college, and was an ice hockey goalie for SUNY Cortland. People had commented on his innate intelligence and problem solving ability since he was a child. So why the self-doubt now? What was at the root of his apparent issue with the test taking? Why the lack of integration and learning, and the limiting beliefs? How would this affect his future?

At that moment of my son's challenge I asked myself what I could do to help improve Mike's performance and his future. What was the real challenge underlying this circumstance? As evolutionary sound frequency entrainment technology innovators, what could we do to help him to improve his performance? Little did I know or understand at that moment, the key to Mike's performance would lie in a little understood area of the human brain known as the frontal lobe.

That day on the phone we created a plan to address Mike's current learning, performance, and consciousness challenge. Mike would travel to our home in Hot Springs, Arkansas on Tuesday August 17th to study for 8 days, and we would schedule an appointment for him to take the actual GMAT on August 25th in Little Rock. I decided to ask my partner Robert Lloy if he would design a technology specifically targeted to accelerate learning and focus and increase intelligence to enhance Mike's GMAT study. Fortunately, he agreed. I realized if we cracked the code on this one, it could help children and adults throughout the world who needed more brainpower and greater performance, in whatever they were seeking to accomplish. I had put this request on the vision board of our company in the previous year, but we had postponed the invention as we had other priorities at the time.

Our plan was to create the Tesla Focus IQube, and for Mike to study in close proximity to the device, while we measured if it accelerated his learning efforts. We would measure whether, in this short period of 8 days, Mike's GMAT score improved. Another measure would be if it enabled him to concentrate for longer periods of time to prepare for the GMAT, instead of becoming discouraged and withdrawing in frustration. Our intention was to develop a new set of sound frequencies that would stimulate the subtle energy of the frontal lobe. As our work is based on the principles of sound entrainment and subtle energy, Mike would entrain with the field of energy and thus activate his frontal lobe, which in theory would accelerate his learning and comprehension of the material.

THE BREAKTHROUGH IN OUR UNDERSTANDING

Our research into the vast field of neuroscience had shown that the frontal lobe held the key to the energy of the brain, the ability to accelerate learning, concentration and enhance intelligence. Many call the frontal lobe the seat of genius or the CEO of the brain (Arntz, William; Chasse, Betsy; Vincente, Mark — "What the Bleep Do We Know!?; Health Communications Inc. Deerfield, FL 2003). It governs will, intent and focus. With greater energy in the frontal lobe and the enhanced intelligence that results, it would be easier to accomplish more with less effort. It seemed like such a simple solution to such a complex problem.

In the interim, in order to grasp what might be going on with Mike, I began to do more research on the brain and consciousness. Although my graduate studies at the University of Chicago had focused on the Psychological Treatment of Individuals, Families and Groups at the School of Social Service Administration, I realized that when my studies were completed over 20 years ago, there was absolutely no attention on the human brain. In my latest research, I recognized that when there is more energy in the frontal lobe, our productivity is naturally enhanced simply by allowing us to concentrate for longer periods of time. I also began to realize that in Mike's 17-year ice hockey career as a goalie, he had received many "pucks to the brain/ helmet" which could have had an effect on the energy and circuitry in his brain and could also impact his ability to integrate complex material.

MIKE'S SHIFT

On the day Mike flew in from New York, Robert had completed the first Tesla Focus IQube. When Mike sat down to resume his GMAT study, we placed the Tesla Focus IQube next to the area where he would study. This would allow him to entrain with the frequencies emanating from the technology and enhance his ability to concentrate. On the first day he took another practice test, and it was around 550. He continued to study continuously for 3 days, taking breaks only for meals and light workouts.

One night after dinner, Mike prepared to take another practice test. It was Sunday night and the GMAT test was Wednesday. I was sitting outside at the pool when I heard Mike jumping up and down and shouting. I went inside to discover that he had obtained a victorious 690 on the practice test! He had broken the barrier. He was beyond ecstatic and so was I. Mike had exceeded his belief of what he could attain. The change in the test score indicated our experimental Tesla Focus IQube had worked to shift and switch on Mike's frontal lobe so he could more fully integrate and apply what he was studying. But would this change endure the stress of the actual testing environment where he would perform without the Tesla Focus IQube?

What surprised me on our drive to Little Rock was that Mike continued to learn. He had no anxiety. When I dropped him off at the Pearson Center for the test, he was confident. Three hours later he emerged from the building, again jumping for joy, and showed me the official test score. He had achieved a 640 on the GMAT. Mike had fulfilled the first goal of his intention - to break the 550 barrier.

THE TURNING POINT

When Mike returned to SUNY armed with his own Tesla Focus IQube for his room, his entire attitude and outlook had changed. He knew that he had broken through his limitations and that his capacity would expand. He had cultivated an attitude of "I am smart enough" from "not smart enough." Due to the increased energy in the frontal lobe, Mike's consciousness of his own potential and capabilities had also shifted. As a result, he studied more, received a 4.1 average, was elected to the Honor Society, and graduated Summa Cum Laude. He was also awarded the Chairs Award for Academic Excellence in Finance. These were all signs that the frontal lobe of Mike's brain was clearly switched on.

THE OUTCOME

Mike continued to prepare for a 2nd GMAT test during his senior year. His goal was to obtain a 700 or above so he could be admitted to his dream program - the Masters in Finance at Vanderbilt University, a program that only admitted those who attained a 700 or higher GMAT score. With the frontal lobe firing in this new way, he achieved his intention. At the second sitting, he received a 710. Mike had increased his GMAT score and realized his dream! On February 7th 2012, he was removed from the waitlist at Vanderbilt University, after the second score of the GMAT, and admitted into the program

What struck me throughout this period was how fulfilling it was as a mother to see Mike's frontal lobe "switched on", and how he became more at peace with himself. It seemed to be a natural unfoldment. At times when he called, I would remark that it felt that I had another son. He was operating at a level that I could only have dreamt of in the past.

Switching on and Actively Developing Your Most Valuable Real Estate: The Frontal Lobe (How you can Apply the Five Secret Keys in Mike's Success Story)

"The frontal lobe makes choices that support our desire for a particular outcome. When we use this part of our brain to its capacity, our behavior matches our purpose, and our actions match our intent – our mind and body are one. How many times have our behavior and purpose matched completely?" *Evolve Your Brain* — Health Communications, Inc. 2007; Joe Dispenza; p. 357

The "Tesla Focus IQube" applies five key activation principles that are essential to enhanced mastery and success. Conscious application of these secrets will amplify and accelerate your results in all endeavors. The premise is that you will do whatever it takes to switch on and actively develop the "Frontal Lobe real estate" that you were naturally endowed with. You may look at this as the most valuable real estate that you possess. The frontal lobe holds the reigns over the emotional self and endows you with the capacity of conscious choice, free will, genius and infinite creativity. With a developed frontal lobe you are unlimited in your potential.

THE FIVE KEY PRINCIPLES TO "SWITCH ON " AND MASTER YOUR FRONTAL LOBE REAL ESTATE

1. Brainwave Entrainment

Brainwave entrainment is any practice, tool or technology that aims to cause brainwave frequencies to align with an external stimulus. The key to entrainment is the frequency-following response. When we are subjected to specific frequencies, we align with this and alter our brainwave state. The use of frequency-based technologies or instruments such as the Tesla Focus IQube allows the brain to entrain with frequencies in the alpha (8-13 cycles) and theta (4-7 cycles) range while simultaneously applying frequencies to stimulate the frontal lobe. When we entrain with this new range of frequencies we naturally shift and experience greater creativity, accelerated learning, and enhanced problem-solving ability. In my personal experience, this "continuous entrainment" opens the doorway to our potential. Entrainment with specified frequencies can be applied for accelerated learning and results in both business and personal domains.

2. The Law of Repetition

Repetition is vitally important to switch on the frontal lobe and re-pattern our responses to allow new learning and behaviors. Brain states are like exercising a muscle. The more you repeat the exercise, the more you switch on the frontal lobe through entrainment. This could be through writing, studying, or creating a product. This allows the creation of new wired neural networks to occur. "Switching on the frontal lobe" once will not create the desired result. It takes time and repetition to create the neurological and behavioral changes that we desire. Repetitive practice creates enduring frontal lobe transformation.

3. The Law of Resonance

Everything has a natural or resonant frequency. Through continuous exposure to a new set of frequencies, one can change the resonance. By introducing Mike to a new set of sound frequencies, we were able to re-pattern his brain and the way that he was learning. Continuous exposure to the stimulus of these frequencies appeared to have increased his mathematical and verbal ability. Your frontal lobe can be switched on and will take on a new resonance when it is exposed to frequencies that are designed to activate it. The quantum leap that Mike was able to take is an excellent illustration of the Law of Resonance. By enhancing Mike's frontal lobe through frequency applications, he was able to "rise to the challenge" and use his brain in a way which enhanced his performance.

4. The Law of Intent
The frontal lobe is the part of the brain that governs firm intention. When we have truly made up our minds to act in a certain way, we activate the frontal lobe. Intention is the most crucial aspect of the frontal lobe.

"The seat of our free will and self determination, the frontal lobe allows us to choose our every thought and action and, in so doing, control our own destiny. When this lobe is active, we focus on our desires, create ideas, make conscious decisions, carry out an intentional course of action, and regulate our behavior. The evolution of the human frontal lobe bestowed on humans a focused, intentional, creative, willful, decisive, purposeful mind, if we will only put it to use." *Evolve Your Brain* — Health Communications, Inc. 2007; Joe Dispenza; p. 140

Act with focused intention and you are naturally activating your frontal lobe. In Mike's case, he had a clear intention in mind and through the activation of the frontal lobe, he was able to concentrate and take action to bring this into manifestation.

5. The Practice of Extreme Neuroplasticity
In the movie Groundhog Day, Bill Murray's character victoriously changes the repetitive behavior that is keeping him stuck in time. Everyone has the same opportunity to adapt, to change and to succeed. Everyone has the potential to alter the brain's wired-together neuronets, transform redundant habits and attain liberation from self-imposed limitations. Neuroplasticity is the word that best describes the brain's innate capacity to make these new connections

and create new opportunities and accomplishments from this!

By learning to use your brain in new ways, you can cultivate an attitude of neuroplasticity, which naturally creates new neural pathways in the brain. With new frequencies, knowledge or instruction the consciousness is rewired and becomes extremely flexible and adaptable to change. Extreme neuroplasticity is the willingness to engage in new ideas, actions, and practices. This "neuroplastic" flexibility is the portal of your evolution. Extreme neuroplasticity = More smarts = Enhanced results.

Change is cumulative and occurs daily when you consciously "switch on" the real estate of your frontal lobe. Through the application of sound frequencies and the principles of brainwave entrainment, repetition, resonance, extreme neuroplasticity, and intention we can rewire ourselves and our children to create an enhanced future.

In Mike's case, he has switched on his frontal lobe and changed his destiny forever. He is now 10 weeks into the program at Vanderbilt and has one job offer as a Financial Analyst at Nissan. He is also in the final interview round for a position at Stephens Inc. - a Fortune 500 company that narrowed down an applicant pool of 1,000 to 40. Mike made a quantum leap into the elevated terrain of his destiny.

On October 12th Mike was picked up in Stephens corporate jet at the Nashville Airport and flown with 39 other applicants to Little Rock, Arkansas---the corporate headquarters of Stephens, Inc. I received a call on Sunday, October 14th, 2012. He had received one of the first offers for a position as a financial analyst. Mike accepted the offer on Tuesday, October 16th, 2012 – 2 years and 2 months after he began his new quest for neuroplasticity. One might ponder what the outcome might have been without this quantum shift in the way that he was using his brain?

This quantum leap has revealed that most of us are capable of brilliantly accomplishing noble tasks if we simply dedicate ourselves to the evolution of our most precious real estate – the frontal lobe. There is a dormant genius and a set of gifts within each of us. Change comes from our simple willingness to switch on and intentionally utilize our innate capability. Using our brain in a new way can result in a quantum leap in our potential and performance.

About Helena

EARLY CAREER, GRADUATE WORK & LIFE MISSION & THE SECRET

Helena Reilly, M.A. is a pioneer and expert in the use of sound frequencies and scalar technology to effect profound transformation. She decided to become a child psychologist at the age of fifteen when it was discovered that she had a unique gift to communicate with children who were experiencing learning and emotional challenges. After completing her graduate work in the Psychological Treatment of Children, Families and Groups at the University of Chicago, she travelled the world in search of a therapeutic modality that effected lasting transformation that actually worked. She discovered the ancient secret that entrainment with sound frequencies facilitated a shift in brainwave states that are the key to all transformation and enhanced productivity. When she met her partner, Robert Lloy, she discovered that he was the master creator of Sacred Scalar Vortex Technology and had been doing amazing research in Sound Frequencies for over 20 years.

PRIVATE PRACTICE & SOUND ENERGETICS

Helena applied Lloy's Voice Activation Hydration System to her Manhattan-based private practice with extraordinary results. The" VAHS" software analyzed the Human Voice and delivered sound frequencies to remove deep stresses. During this time, she created a therapeutic system and wrote her book "Sound Energetics" based on her client's transformations. She also combined the VAHS with hypnosis to help her clients attain amazing results in their personal and professional lives. She was interviewed on numerous television and radio talk shows including Carol Martin's CNBC "Alive and Wellness." Her specialty was dealing with gifted creative people whose desire was to remove unconscious blocks to success. She frequently lectured and travelled and facilitated large groups during this phase of her career.

CO-FOUNDER OF SMART TECHNOLOGY ASSOCIATION/CO-CREATOR OF TESLA IQUBES

In 2002 Helena left her private practice to join Robert Lloy full time. Since that time they applied this knowledge to co-create the Tesla IQubes (Focus, Theta Love and Tesla) each synergistically combining scalar vortex action, sound frequencies, inert noble gases (such as xenon), LEDs, and structured water. The Tesla IQubes are based on constant entrainment with coherent fields of energy.

She is the president and co-founder of Smart Technology Association. She is now travelling to teach and introduce the Tesla Iqubes to increase human potential and remove the deep stresses that prevent individuals from actualizing their highest potential. She also designed and implemented the certification program for Sound Coaches and is a Certified Sound Coach.

More information on the Tesla IQubes can be found on Helena's websites and contact information:
www.teslaiqubes.com;
E-mail: Helena@moresmarts.com
805-456-2172
Facebook: helenareilly9
SKYPE: helenareilly

CHAPTER 17

THE DETERMINED DOZEN

BY SHANE MEREM

After successfully designing, managing and launching over 8,000 web applications and e-commerce stores -- I want to share with you some of the most important factors that will contribute to your success.

I say "contribute" because even under great circumstances, a vast majority of e-commerce businesses fail. Just like any type of small business, why does one coffee shop fail when another one in the same location thrives? Why do franchise coffee shops have a better chance of success than someone with less experience doing it alone?

The answer is simple. A franchise will offer known working strategies to each franchise owner. That will significantly improve their chance of success. That being said -- any business requires a lot of work. Period. And not everyone is cut out to be a business owner.

For as long as I can remember, there are people who envision a website like a magic lamp. You just need to get your hands on one and your dreams will come true. Just buy a site and it will start making money.

There is nothing further from the truth. You buy a website and you just got in line behind hundreds of thousands of your worldwide competitors. Now what?

A web-based business does offer some advantages. First, many require less of an up front investment. Compare maybe $10,000.00 (or less) to a brick-and-mortar start up of $200,000.00. Also your potential customer base is worldwide.

In my opinion the proverbial "Ma and Pa shops" have not disappeared. They just went global. You can still get great service from small business owners who truly care about their customers. Right from your own home.

I could write thousands of pages of technical facts. The technical stuff is really the least significant aspect of a successful website. I have identified six absolutely critical things you need to succeed online.

- A PROFITABLE product
- A "GOOD" website design. Not a "great" one. (I'll explain later)
- YOU must mind your website (not some tech guy)
- MAKE the SEARCH ENGINES understand your business!
- DON'T ignore security.
- Be PATIENT!

1. "A Profitable Product"

A profitable product sounds like common sense. It's the first and most common conversations with business owners.

Search engines like Google work on a page-by-page basis. Under most circumstances they don't view your website as a "store." They are trying to match a specific page to a specific search phrase. It's unrealistic to expect every product in your brand new store to pop up when a person does their search. So if you must focus on a small subset of items -- start marketing your highest profit items first. Over time as you start selling products, you can start working on other products and categories.

2. "A GOOD web design — not a great one"

You need a "good" web design. Anyone telling you, has never helped their customer become financially successful. Your design is a tool just like anything else.

Let's think about a restaurant you recently visited for the first time. You walked in and looked around. In less than one second you have determined if this restaurant is clean and looks "nice." After that -- you sit down and look at the menu. Do they have what you want to eat?

I cannot illustrate this point any simpler. Most of you don't remember if the chairs were metal or wood. You don't remember what shade of yellow their sign is. You spent an entire second to make a YES/NO decision. Now it's all about the menu and how good the food tastes!

I'm not saying you shouldn't take pride in your website design. I'm just saying that nobody cares what shade of grey is in your background. I have watched hundreds of projects delayed in the design phase because our customer obsessed about a color, a photo, or how many pixels wide a border is. If you want to build a website for your own "vanity," then go for it! It has nothing to do with how much money you make. I'll prove it. Take a look at: http://www.craigslist.com . It's got to be one of the ugliest websites ever created. Yet, it is responsible for millions of dollars in sales.

3. "YOU must mind your website"

Replace your IT person without becoming one! There are too many solutions out there that offer zero programming ways to manage your own website. My most successful clients manage their entire website on their own. You may be too busy to do it yourself -- that's OK. Your website should still be easy to manage by your average employee – your receptionist, your shipping staff or your sales staff. In most cases a dedicated IT person should not be required to run a successful e-commerce website. And you should always know how your system works. You must know what to expect before expecting someone else to help you with your e-commerce website.

4. "Make the search engines understand your business!"

You can't wait or hope it will happen. You can't trick the search engines into understanding your business (though people will try to say they can). You must use technology outlined by the search engines to your own advantage. Let me clarify a few terms for my next explanation.

The term "Search Engine Friendly" simply means -- Can a search engine visit your home page and successfully crawl from page to page until it has read every word and every product on your website? It has nothing to do with the position of your search results.

The term "Search Engine Optimized" means your "Search Engine Friendly" website has been edited following known rules and advice that should help you move to a better position in the search engine results. You must have a "Search Engine Friendly" e-commerce website to optimize it — making it "Search Engine Optimized." You cannot do one without the other.

A fast-talking salesperson might speak as if the two are the same. Make sure you ask for clarification when evaluating an e-commerce website company.

Not all sites are "Search Engine Friendly." Because search engines like Google wanted to help people who had already built websites, "Google Sitemaps" was created.

"Google Sitemaps" was defined originally by Google to allow a programmer to build a special document that describes every page and product on your website just in case your site was not "Search Engine Friendly."

That specification continues to say that you should update this sitemap file every time you update your website, so that Google can always stay up to date with your pages and products!

This has become a standard for other search engines including Yahoo! and Bing. Using "Google Sitemap" technology on your website is proven to make a difference in your search engine results!

Do not confuse this technical document with a page on your site named "Sitemap." They are not the same. Carefully listen to what your salesperson is talking about. Very few e-commerce web design companies will educate you about this very important part of bringing customers to your website. The reason they won't mention it is because many "web designers" aren't technically capable of programming this option for you.

Another important technology you must have to compete is "Google Merchant Center" compatibility (formerly known as "Froogle"). "Google Merchant Center" is designed to assure your products are properly explained to a search engine. However this focuses specifically on your products. It is another feature you must insist is included in your e-commerce website. Google offered this for free in the past. They are starting to require some paid advertising to take advantage of it. It's a strong way to get your products to take hold in the search engines.

Finally, you just might need a search engine expert to give you some advice. Every successful e-commerce business come to a point where they need some help understanding what's going on with their search results. Especially where you are trying to beat millions of competing websites.

What DOES NOT help your search engine results? It is just as important to know what not to do when it comes to marketing your website in the search engines.

Constant site submissions. One of the most misunderstood concepts. YES - Just about every low-end e-commerce website company says they will resubmit your site to all sorts of search engines every month. NO - It does not help you.

Your site needs to be submitted only one time. Submit your site with one of the major search engines like Google or Yahoo! That's it! Any other search engine that matters WILL find your site. Multiple search submission services only assure that your mailbox will be spammed daily.

Multiple domain names. Though it's true that you should select your domain name carefully, you can get into trouble if you purchase a bunch of domain names and simply point them to your website.

It may even handicap your search results! There is a right way to take advantage of buying extra domain names. Make sure you consult a search engine expert before using multiple domain names to promote your website so you stay out of trouble. Make sure you choose a search engine expert that promotes a "content" based approach. Stay away from so-called experts that claim to have some "secrets" or "tricks" and only ask for a large sum of money. A good marketing approach will require you to provide content and articles to support his efforts.

5. "DON'T ignore security"

Security! Unfortunately most companies learn about security the hard way. Just when you start making some sales. Just when you sit back and relax for just a moment to enjoy your new online business – it happens.

You wake up and your website home page is defaced with a "Turkish Hacker Gang Sign"! Don't laugh. I've seen it happen!

You can design a site to perform a function, OR you can design a site to perform a function securely. There are two very distinct methods of programming. You MUST always choose the secure method from the ground up.

Think about buying an automatic garage door opener. You take for granted that if a child is in the doorway when the garage door closes, the safety feature will immediately stop the door and tell it to open back up. You probably couldn't find an automatic garage door opener that doesn't have this important safety feature.

If e-commerce websites were garage door openers – very few have the necessary security to protect you!

Why would you purchase a website without the necessary security? You wouldn't. Security is more difficult to understand in the e-commerce business. Everyone offers a "SSL Certificate" and a pretty lock on the browser to show your customers that your site is secure. Security is so much more than that!

How does anyone get away with selling insecure sites? The majority of websites won't generate enough traffic or sales to become a target. If you can't be found on the web -- then you can't be a target. As soon as customers can find your website -- you may become a target for hackers too.

Credit card security. PCI Compliance is a new standard that the "Card Brands" (i.e., Visa, MasterCard, etc) created to hold merchants account-able for credit card fraud. Now you can be fined if you are not following the latest PCI DSS Standard. Suffice it to say that you must make sure your e-commerce website complies with these standards – as well as your internal network and policies.

For larger businesses, failing a PCI Compliance audit can result in fi-nancial penalties and possibly termination of your account. I became a PCI QSA just to make sure I could properly consult our clients and developers. It's important.

6. "Patience"

Patience is last but not least on my list. I have real-life customers run-ning profitable e-commerce websites with millions of dollars in yearly revenue. These customers all have a few things in common. First, they have everything I outlined above. Next, they hard every day on their e-commerce website. Finally, they realize it takes time to become suc-cessful. If it was easy – everyone would be millionaires!

About Shane

Shane Merem was one of those kids that took everything apart. He remembers taking a robotics class at age 10. The top of his Christmas list was a Radio Shack 2001 circuits project kit — EVERY YEAR. In his words, "So yeah, I was a geek before it was cool to be a geek."

His first passion was digital electronics. Building circuits from scratch. After successfully working in that field until his early 20's running the service division of a large automotive electronics company, he boldly started his own business and his real education began. Shane spent some years in computers when the DOS era was strong and the text version of Windows (version 3.1) was becoming extinct.

Shane found the engineering and software side of things were still his favorite. He had a reputation for taking on projects in areas in which he had no expertise. After buying $500.00 worth of books and software, he would complete the project successfully and within budget. Some projects were small and some were huge. He still has piles of books around his office and home.

Shane formed a company named Magnus Software in 1995 specializing in POS (Point of sale) software for grocery store cash registers. In the same time frame, he had just started dabbling with dynamic, data-driven web-based applications. This was technology that the average Joe had not heard of. It was a perfect opportunity for him.

He spent a couple of years selling websites door to door. The Internet was so new that most prospects threw him out with the most common objection — *"The Internet is just a fad, it won't be around long."* You can imagine how long ago that was! Over half the business population were non-believers! He has sold and built websites for a long time.

Magnus Software spent the end of the 1990's building 1 to 3 sites per month. They were 'big money' sites for 'big money' businesses. They were the only companies that could afford to do it and business was good. Lisa, Shane's wife, ran the business side of things while they both earned terrific customers and a great reputation in the web industry.

Nothing lasts forever – as he hit the year 2000 and into 2001, around the "Dot Bomb" era he found he couldn't give away a website. Everyone was sick from losing enormous amounts of money in the "Dot Com" stock market investments. He had to come up with a plan. Instead of a few customers paying big money, he knew he needed a second business model that everyone could use and most could afford. That product was named "Website Forge." Approaching his fourth decade of life, Shane is known for building million dollar sites with Website Forge and Magnus Software.

Shane and Lisa enjoy time with their three kids in Fowlerville, Michigan, not far from where they grew up.

CHAPTER 18

SEALING THE CRACKS IN YOUR FINANCIAL PATHWAY

BY STEVE SEXTON

Do you plan to retire someday? Most likely you do. Maybe you want to retire by the ocean, or on a fishing lake in Tennessee, or you want to travel. Perhaps in addition to retiring well, you would like to leave something for your children or grandchildren. Whatever your plan, you should have assembled a group of trusted advisors; your financial planner, your CPA and your estate attorney to handle wills and trusts—and I hope that they are all on the same page of your plan.

People rely on their primary care doctors to coordinate their healthcare among many health professionals, specialists, and pharmacists. A coordinated plan can save lives when one person looks at the big picture and sees the treatment from all vantage points. Where treatments overlap, overmedication can occur causing more harm than good. The same is true of retirement investments. By not having a process or believing in myths or having too many advisors who do not coordinate their treatment, things fall through the cracks. It can be catastrophic to assume that the CPA, or attorney, or the financial advisor knows exactly what your goals are. They are not likely working in unison. Add to that the fact that most investors don't have a process in place for filtering out financial myths, or for determining how much they are actually earning on investments after fees and taxes, and you have a perfect storm for retirement disaster.

There are three things to consider for ensuring your retirement portfolio matches your retirement vision: **Purpose, Process, and Profit**. Purpose varies from person to person, as retirement goals are not one-size-fits-all. First, we establish what is your investment purpose or goal. Second, we use our three-step review process for looking at every aspect of your portfolio from percentage return on each fund to the tax burden your children will bear when inheriting your life's savings. Finally, we ascertain that your investments garner the profit you expect they will, so you are not living with the myth of a 6% return when your net profit after fees and taxes is only 2%.

We use a three-step review or "discovery" process to profile our client's investment decisions. We begin with a full review of the client's personal financial situation and determine how their income flows onto their tax return? How is everything on that tax return associated with everything else; how does it intersect? What are the issues on your tax return that are compounding the amount of money you have to pay in taxes? What strategies can be implemented that will lower or eliminate your taxes? We review your income streams. Are you using them effectively and efficiently? What are your issues with long-term care? What are your estate and charitable desires? How do you want to see things move off to the ones you love? The wonderful benefit of our three-step review is that it applies to any financial decision or concern you have. The three-step process can help you stop your money from falling through the cracks and help assure that any major financial decision is right for you. In other words, learn the questions to ask before making any financial decision and identify ways to assure your decisions are in your best interest.

Many people, whether doctors, lawyers, teachers or construction workers, spend 30, 40, 50 years becoming successful at their profession. They likely made mistakes early on that cost them money, because they lacked the insider knowledge acquired though experience. If you are a business owner, you likely remember that early on in your business, you spent, oh, $5,000 on a marketing program that did not work out and you have only found out later that it was not successful because you didn't have the demographics right. When we retire, we move into a new career where we do not know the business. A new retiree may not know what questions to ask his advisors, attorney, CPA, or financial advisor? Are your financial advisors actually talking with each other? Have you quantified the true cost of your investments--the impact of these fees, taxes and charges on your income taxes not only now, but also in the future? What about your estate taxes?

Our job as financial advisors is to help our clients get a handle on those things: to see if it is actually happening to them, so when they look at their holdings and investment portfolio, they can see if money is falling through the cracks. Then, when they look forward into the future, they can then determine the best course of action and make decisions that are in line with the client's wants and desires. In doing so, clients find ways to assure the decisions they make are in their best interests.

Here is the story of a client, named Jeannette, who might be very much like you. Jeannette is 70 years old, comes from a mid-size town on the West Coast of the United States, and is a wonderful woman. Her passions are her daughter, her son, and her grandkids. Jeannette wants to make sure everybody is happy and healthy, but Jeannette has financial concerns. Despite having had the same financial advisor, certified public accountant, and estate-planning attorney for the last 30 years, Jeannette became concerned that the economy in our country and the potential increase of taxes would adversely affect her retirement health. She is concerned, rightfully so, that her nest egg is not going to last as long as she once thought it would. Jeannette arrived at our office voicing concerns about things like, "Hey, what if something happens to me? How am I going to take care of this or that?" Most importantly, Jeannette wants to make sure that her assets continue to grow. She wants to make sure that when she walks out on life that all of those assets transfer to her children with the least amount of taxes. She does not want to pay any more than her fair share to the IRS.

In our discussions with Jeannette, we went through a discovery process. We wanted to understand her personal situation, personal financial situation, and things that are important to her. It turns out that Jeannette and her husband had always worked on their financial planning together with an advisor for their investments, so they trusted in that advisor. They asked questions here or there, and worked with a C.P.A. who prepared their taxes. When Jeannette's husband passed away, she kept the same advisors and expected them to be managing her interests. The primary reason Jeannette and her son-in-law came into our office was they had moved and left their trusted advisors behind, so they were looking for a new advisor. When they spoke to us, Jeannette was primarily concerned about passing on her assets and making certain those assets last as long as her children do.

As with all clients, we applied five critical questions to every investment Jeannette has to determine her investment purpose and see:

1. How they affect her personal financial situation not only now but in the future?

2. How do they affect her taxes--meaning how is all this investment associated with her income taxes? Do they compound her taxes; do they cause her to pay more taxes than she needs to?

3. How do they affect her income? Is she in a position where she's using her income streams ineffectively?

4. What is her risk comfort? Is she comfortable with the risk and does she understand the risk that she is taking on?

5. How do all these investments transition off to the ones she loves?

In reviewing Jeannette's situation, we discovered that Jeannette is earning about $80,000 a year per her income tax return. It turns out that she is only spending about $50,000 a year. That means Jeannette just found out she is paying taxes on money she's not even spending and that means she is being very inefficient from a tax income standpoint. Then we talked further about the investments that she has. We learned that she has a mutual fund portfolio--more of a bond fund portfolio really--and then she has a number of fixed annuities, variable annuities, and some stocks. Her portfolio looks like most people's portfolios in the United States.

The big difference for Jeannette is her advisor is charging her 1% on all of these accounts and meets with her infrequently. There is nothing wrong with her advisor collecting his 1%, except that Jeannette's annuity is a fixed annuity. A fixed annuity operates just like a CD; it has a specified term and a guaranteed, fixed return. Her fixed annuities started out earning 4% and 5% 10-12 years ago, but every 3 or 4 years when these came due, the rate reset and now they're earning only 2% or 3%, and in fact, the average return on her fixed annuities was 2.5%. Jeannette wasn't paying attention to the fact her advisor was charging her

1%, meaning she was effectively earning only 1.5% on her fixed annuities and was not outpacing inflation. Adding in the impact of inflation, she was actually *losing* 2% each year due to the depreciation of dollars. Now that also meant that her advisor was charging her to manage an account that didn't really need managing. If you have a fixed account, why should you give out a 20, 30, 40, or 50% of it to the advisor when they do not have to do anything other than fill out paperwork?

Additionally, Jeannette had variable annuities, which contain mutual funds, bond funds, and fixed accounts. Variable annuities charge fees; they are internal fees that most people don't see and most people don't know about, but they take away from your return. When we talk to the variable annuity companies, we find that there is a Mortality & Expense fee of 1.5%. Moreover, there is an administrative fee of 0.15%. Then there is a sub-account fee of 1.6%, so her fees are already over 3% and there was still another fee called a death benefit fee that was charging another 1%. All told, Jeannette paid almost 4.25% in fees on her variable annuities. Talk about money seeping through the cracks!

Jeannette had this concept that her variable annuities would earn her at least 6%. When we studied the returns of the variable annuities from the time she had them–over 20 years–she had actually only earned about 2%. After she paid her advisor, Jeannette was really earning only 1%. Jeannette had an unrealistic expectation of earning 6% because she didn't know about the element of the unknown fees or the internal fees that go with the variable annuities. As a result, her returns were not even coming close to meeting her expectations; they were not fulfilling her purpose. Furthermore, of her entire portfolio, we determined that in the last three years Jeannette had only earned a little over 1%. Jeannette became very, very frustrated when she realized her assets are actually losing value by virtue of depreciation and inflation – at a time when she thought her financial needs satisfied.

The next step in our process was to review Jeannette's estate. We quickly determined that if we stuck with the mutual funds, or did something capital gain related--because she has a trust--those assets would step up in value when she passes away and her children or grandchildren would pay no taxes. All those fixed, variable annuities and IRA's were a different story. Back in the early days, those variable annuities and those fixed annuities were earning 6% and 7% when everything was going really,

really, really well. As such, she built up a little cash, some IRAs, and a significant amount of interest income in those accounts.

If she died tomorrow, her kids would end up paying $300,000 in taxes, and that shocked her. She said, "I don't want them to pay $300,000 in taxes, and besides, I have a trust that takes care of this." Jeannette did not fully understand that a trust, which takes care of Probate and Estate Taxes and anything that's capital gain related, steps up in value upon death. A person's IRA and annuities all have interest income build up, and therefore are taxable upon death, or on the transfer of those products to somebody else.

To eliminate Jeannette's tax time bomb, we found an annuity account that would still enable her to tax defer her growth and, for a small fee, eliminate the taxes at her passing. Yes, there is a fee. Jeannette felt the fee was less expensive than life insurance. Paying a few thousand dollars a year while still earning a return until she passed would save her children $300,000 to $500,000 in taxes from the transition of her annuities. Now she has an estate plan that is in line with her wants and desires.

The big issue for Jeannette and her taxes is that she did not understand why she had capital gains in the first place when she had never sold any of her mutual funds or bond funds. We explained that the only things held inside a mutual fund are stocks and bonds. When the money manager wants to retain his gains or reallocate, he sells off funds that have been gaining so he can keep their earnings as high as possible. People naturally see that as a positive, so they invest in the mutual fund.

Nevertheless, when you hold the mutual fund you receive a 1099 for the gains in those mutual funds and the gains of those stocks inside those mutual funds. For Jeannette, that was $10,000. How does that relate to her tax return? As it turns out, Jeannette was paying 15% in Federal taxes just like all of us in 2010--that means $1500 just on Federal taxes she was going to have to pay the second she walked into her CPA's office. On top of which, her State taxes equaled another 5%, therefore, she was actually paying $2,000 a year for this turnover *inside* her funds. In fact, we had determined that over the last three years, she had actually paid more than $2,000 a year without realizing it. This big phantom tax doesn't affect only Jeannette. Throughout the United States in 2010, people paid in $25 billion dollars in this phantom income tax alone.

Many people like Jeanette do not have a process in place for making financial decisions. They have never quantified the cost of investments, filtered myths or misinformation, misconceptions or unrealistic expectations, and are making decisions that are flawed and misaligned with their wants and desires. That's why they have an uneasy feeling or have the 800 lb. Gorilla on their back when it comes to their retirement.

Recent surveys of affluent Americans consistently tell us that their major frustration is their advisor should be more proactive about future issues that might affect their financial well-being. According to insurance industry surveys and research, 80% of the people who purchase fixed index or variable annuities do so for the purchase of income, but they end up never taking that income. As a result, that income transfers to their beneficiaries, and becomes interest income build up that can hit beneficiaries with a time bomb of taxes.

Is this happening to you? Historically you may have purchased financial or insurance products and then later found out how they affected your taxes and investment plan. The correct course of action is to discover your needs and build a proper plan first. What we don't know or the questions we do not think to ask or clarify may be costing us severely. By finding out how you arrive at financial decisions, we can determine if your process is perhaps flawed. Correcting a flawed process enables a person to match their true needs and desires through more informed financial decisions. Each investment product has a place and a specific purpose where it may fit properly into someone's retirement planning, but without a complete review of the personal situation, risk tolerance, income needs, tax situation, long-term care needs, estate and desires, no one can or should have an accurate opinion whether a specific product is right for you.

Discovering your true desires and needs, your investment purpose, is the first step you should take. Use an educated process to find the right combination of products to meet your profit needs – while not allowing money to seep through the cracks of your financial pathway.

About Steve

Steve Sexton helps clients take control of their finances by identifying areas where money is "falling through the cracks" in their financial and estate plans both now and in the future. He does this by asking questions that most people don't think to ask, or don't know to ask. Then he helps clients redirect those dollars to travel, children, charities, kitchen remodels or whatever is important to them.

Steve developed a comprehensive, yet simple three-step review process of tax, income, and investment monies, which enables clients to find literally thousands of dollars every year that they did not know they were losing.

Steve is the well-known host of the *Money Minute* segment on Channel 6 (CW) and other financial features on the *San Diego Daily Living Show*. Steve hosts his own Financial and Lifestyle Radio Show Sunday mornings on KCBQ/1170am and shares his expertise on various television, radio and print media outlets throughout Southern California and nationally.

CHAPTER 19

EXECUTION STYLE

BY JUSTIN POTTS

My wife asked in utter amazement, "Are you really going to title your chapter of this book *Execution Style Business?*" After she asked the question, she quickly knew what my answer would be and the type of response I would give her. WHY NOT? I have been known to share with people one of the most needed and talked-about topics in the entrepreneur's mind and struggles – and that is Execution. We entrepreneurs have the ability to come up with many ideas and lots of great thinking and never get where we would like to go, because the next great *thing* steals the thunder. One of our biggest frustrations is not achieving the level of success we would like to achieve because of our ADD and Highly Distracted minds.

There is an answer and it is NOT drugs! I am going to share with you a portion of my formula for what allowed me to handle and become an *Execution Style Business*! …If you dare to read!

WHAT'S YOUR GAME

After being accepted into this awesome book as one of the featured co-authors, my next several weeks were about to get extremely crazy. If it wasn't for the *Execution Style Business* that I operate which allows me to travel when and where I want I wouldn't have been able to write this chapter and operate the several different entities that I do.

By the way, this is the exact *Execution Style Business* that has allowed me to earn millions in only four small years and live the life that I always wanted, dreamed about and never knew how to obtain. This piece that I am going to share with you is exactly that. A piece of my formula I feel is extremely valuable to anyone, no matter if you are highly distracted like myself or if you are laser-focused. You still must employ an *Execution Style Business* if you want the rest of the puzzle to come together.

Do you feel like you are a sports player? Seriously? Do you TRULY feel like you are a sports player no different than any other professional sports player? I do! I strongly feel you should as well. You may be asking yourself why I feel like I am a professional sports player. The answer to this question stems from the word Execution. Each and every day the professional sports players of this world must <u>execute</u> in every facet of their day in order to win. And with winning (or losing) comes a great payday with lots of earnings and even bonuses. What game do you play? What's your sport? My sport is the sport of business and I am challenged every day to build my brand, start new ventures and *execute* at one hundred percent.

This is the exact topic I am going to be sharing with you in this chapter and I hope you enjoy. But first, I want to share with you a little about where I was only four short years ago with business, family and distractions. Before I get to the *Execution Style Business* section of my formula, which will answer your questions of how to Execute if you have much on your plate like myself; my past is going to paint a picture of where you may be or may have been and paint a picture of where you can go and the dreams you can be capturing.

I WAS DEFEATED

Four short years ago exactly to this exact month of writing this chapter, I pulled into a local gas station in the town where I was slaved to a J.O.B. and was only able to put $5 dollars of gas, on a credit card that was maxed out, in our little cracker box Nissan car. I had my wife and newborn baby, which was born 3 weeks prior, with me and I had to explain to them that Daddy was unable to provide and we may be unable to go anywhere the next day. How embarrassing! How humiliating! Can you relate?

We were poor and living on little income, dead broke, recipients of the state Medicaid and Government Food Stamp programs, stressed out, and feeling trapped by what the J.O.B. (Just Over Broke) society was delivering us. This was NOT how I planned my life to unfold and it was not how

I dreamed it would be when I was a child. By far, it is not how I wanted to live life and enjoy life with a beautiful wife and a new-born child.

Growing up in a middle class family with household income of roughly $50,000 a year, I did not grow up with money overflowing, and didn't even grow up with parents who went to college. My sister and I were the first individuals to ever attend four years of college from both sides of our extended family. I knew nothing about starting a business and had no clue that I could even be in ownership of my own business. I thought that was just for the big boys (aka: Fortune 500's).

The only thing I had going for me was I dreamed big starting from birth and began working on a farm in fourth grade. Back where I am from, they call this hard work university at a young age. These two things along with a loving family that always provided and a Lord that is always in control, was the beginning of the "new beginning" in re-inventing myself, my family and my future.

I began writing this chapter for you sitting on a beach in the Caribbean ocean, near the Virgin Islands and off the coast of beautiful Puerto Rico. Days before starting this chapter, my entire family including my new-born baby who is now four years young, and myself were snorkeling off the beautiful reef that separates the Caribbean Ocean and the Atlantic Ocean, living the *Execution Style Business* lifestyle. I had to nurture my arm after being stung by a jellyfish; however, it's worth the sting in order to now live a completely different lifestyle from the simple success formula I developed.

FORMULA STEP #4 – EXECUTE PERSISTENTLY

So based on what I have accomplished and how I accomplished freedom through my avenue of success, there are six steps to my formula to achieving this success and freedom. This specific formula I developed takes place with six coordinated steps and has added sub-categories that help develop your avenue for success and help create success and the life you have always wanted.

The fourth step of my formula is "Execute Persistently." Execution is not a simple process and has five separate tasks that must happen and must continue to happen. I will share those five separate steps after I share a great definition with you.

Execution: The Manner, Style, or Result Of Performance.

EXECUTE PERSISTENTLY

The way Execution takes place does not just happen by taking action. There is a Manner, a Style and a Result of Performance that takes place by the PROPER Execution. The best way to have Proper Execution is with a formula that leads to proper Execution. In return, with proper Execution you should end with Overflowing Success!

The five steps that encompass Execution are as follows.

1. Task Yourself

In order to know exactly what you are doing from hour-to-hour and day-to-day, you must task yourself. This may be extremely difficult for some people to think about because you are already tasked. You are tasked by a boss, an employer, a spouse, or anything else that holds you captive from being able to task yourself. Tasking is a deep concept as well. There are hourly tasks. There are daily tasks. There are weekly tasks. I will keep going... keep thinking farther out! There are monthly tasks, quarterly tasks, yearly tasks and even tasks that may reach out as far as three or more years. You must task in order to accomplish. If you don't accomplish them, you will always be going back to your tasks to see exactly where you failed yourself. It is easy to fail yourself and there should always be a reprimand for this negative action. Be sure to reward yourself when you accomplish a large bucket of tasks. Every task should have a deadline for you to accomplish by, and make sure you reach this deadline.

2. Plan

You may be wondering what the difference between Tasking and Planning may be. I had to find my own difference and it worked wonders for my success and me. Tasking is a general list of what needs to happen. Planning takes it to the next level just prior to the "DO" and allows you to separate out the differences of each task on an individual level. You may only need to Plan three items for the "DO" on one task; however, you may need to have twenty "DO" steps on some other task. This Plan of "DO" or Action allows you to know exactly what you MUST do in order to call it a "Success". This is where you get the chance to be very specific with lots of detail and not hold anything back on what you think it will take in order to accomplish each task. This is fun! It allows you to be Creative and use your imagination in great detail. Just like the Tasks – your Plan list should have a specific deadline for you to accomplish them by and make sure you reach this deadline.

3. Do

This is where you "Do" the "Plan" that details the "Tasks." How awesome! Other people may call this the Action step; however, as you can see – there is more that needs to happen than just the point of Action. That is why it is fully encompassing and a part of my *Execution Style Business,* and it is the reason why I call it the "DO"!

4. Re-Visit

In order to keep up with the "Do" of your business, you must obviously have the first three Formula steps and the last two formula steps; however, you must Re-Visit the Tasks and the Plan in order to keep adjusting your progress and keep obtaining success. Do not take this step lightly. This is important because you must Re-Visit your Tasks and Plan just like you must revisit other parts of the formula. Most people forget this step and it is amazing at how this one broken window can make all the difference. You lose sight, you lose direction and you lose motivation. Your own Tasks and Plan are motivation for "DO" in order to create success. This is key!

5. Prove You to YOU

Warning! Do NOT take this the wrong way! This is not for you to brag, boast or flaunt your success to others. This is to keep you on track and to do exactly what I mentioned above in a previous paragraph. Reward yourself for accomplishment and reprimand yourself for failure. You must keep your own self in check and you must give yourself deadlines and success levels. Make sure you again stay to your Tasks and Plan, and accomplish these by the deadline dates. These deadline dates are for you to Prove You to YOU and to set yourself into the GAME journey. This Prove You to YOU is what sets the stage for your GAME-like experience and is what keeps you competitive with YOU. To obtain success you don't need to be competitive with others – all you need is to be competitive with yourself. Prove You to YOU!

WHERE TO BEGIN

It is difficult for me to tell you where to begin if you are having a struggle similar to my experiences because I am only able to cover one step out of my six step formula. Feel free to go to: www.ChangeInWealth. com to receive a free video that will break down this Formula Step #4 and give you complete details to the other five steps in the formula. Believe me, I still have my struggles, and the best thing for me to do is to continuously go back to my six step formula and re-evaluate every step on every project in order to make sure I am staying inline with my desired outcomes. A distracted mind is hard to overcome and you must have structure. This six step formula for success has been the one thing that has allowed me to go from dead broke and poor to now living the life I had always dreamed of and have always desired.

Massive results can be obtained with Massive steps. Massive steps can be taken with Massive knowledge. Massive knowledge makes all the difference!

To your success – I "cheers" with you!

About Justin

Justin Potts, also known as the creator of the DIVE-IN Success Formula™, is an entrepreneur, doctor, inventor, and owner of multiple businesses. Justin has been developing and inventing for many years and over the last four years has perfected the DIVE-IN Success Formula™ that has allowed him to achieve success in an extremely distracted world and distracted mind.

Being a student of ADD, Justin had to develop a program that would have a step-by-step process for him to follow in order to obtain the desired outcomes and results he was looking for. One of the key differences to his DIVE-IN Success Formula™ is that he had to create it "on his own" since he didn't even know how to get a success coach early in his career. This DIVE-IN Success Formula™ has been used by other businesses in order to streamline their process and aid in the delivery of success. Justin doesn't believe success will come with a genie handing you a bottle. Some people believe all you must do is "wish upon a star" and Justin tends to think differently.

Justin does not believe the economy is in a recession. He believes the only people affected by the recession are the ones living in the recession. The DIVE-IN Success Formula™ creatively allows people to use what the outsiders call a "down economy" in order to create massive wealth for themselves.

To learn more about Justin Potts and the DIVE-IN Success Formula™, How to Change the Direction of Your Life with 6 Proven Steps, and how you can receive a free video on Formula Step #4 and a great way to obtain the remaining five Formula Steps, make sure you check out: www.ChangeInWealth.com. This will give you the insight on how to create your ideal lifestyle and live the life you have always dreamed about… no different than Justin has done for himself, his family and his business.

www.ChangeInWealth.com

CHAPTER 20

THE POWER OF ~~BIG~~ MASSIVE GOALS
—CLIMBING MOUNTAINS, SLAYING WOLVES AND ACHIEVING MASSIVE SUCCESS

BY DUSTIN DART

You deserve to have massive success in all aspects of your life – Here's how.

YOUR ULTIMATE POWER

A few big questions: What do you want to become? What do you want to achieve in life? What's holding you back?

Big secret: You hold in your possession the most important aspect for achieving success – the power of decision. Where will your decisions take you? What will your decisions help you achieve?

Decisions hold massive power and will determine everything you become and achieve in life…good or bad.

We're going to go over the impact of decisions, how to ensure you make the most of your life, and we're going to be climbing mountain peaks, slaying wolves and more. Let's get started!

THE BIG REGRET

The impact of our decisions is massive. We've all decided doing things we thought were amazing or great made us happy, and we've also made decisions that we weren't so happy about.

Among the worst things someone could say is, "I should have, I could have or I would have." These are the words and phrases of regret. We've all said them at some points of our life. I think these words are tragic – regret is tragic.

Your life, your direction, what you become and what you attain are all in your hands. You have control – you have the ultimate power. It is ultimately your DECISION. Once you understand it is your decision alone to do and be what you want, you have the ultimate power.

There are three ways you can view the decisions you make in your life – each level being more desirable than the other:

1 – With regret

2 – Understand the lessons each decision has taught us

3 – With satisfaction you did the boldest and bravest thing you could do

Level one is a complete waste of time – don't let yourself spend any energy with regret…it's tragic. What you can do instead, when you've made a decision you wish you hadn't (this is unavoidable), is to learn the powerful lesson each decision and outcome has to offer you…this is how you grow.

Now here's the kicker – our time is short. Someday the lights are going to turn off. At that point, the big tragedy would be to have regrets and not have learned the lessons you could have. I know it's heavy, but this mindset can help propel you to levels of success you normally wouldn't have achieved.

For example, whenever you're making a decision large or small – think about this… Which decision would you regret more? – and even more powerful – What decision would you be most proud of?

This is an extremely powerful formula to use on a daily basis to lead you to success and satisfaction in life. Now let's go over how you can design the most successful and satisfying life you possibly can.

THE PATHS YOU CHOOSE LEAD TO YOUR DESTINY – CHOOSE WISELY!

The goals you have are the paths that you choose and will lead to your ultimate destiny of regret, mediocrity or massive success. The three levels of outcomes we discussed earlier correlate to the paths and goals that you CHOOSE.

What type of journey do you want to have in life? Most people have no idea what they want out of life. If you don't choose it, it will be chosen for you. And it most likely won't be what you'd really want. Let's look at the three paths you can choose to follow.

Level 1 – THE PAVED ROAD: This path would be like a paved road. This path is the easiest path you can choose and the path that the vast majority of people make. Unfortunately this path is full of regret and it's most likely the path you're walking down right now.

This is a familiar road and you aren't going to need to stretch yourself much to arrive at the destination it's going to take you – mediocrity!

Level 2 – THE DIRT ROAD: The dirt road is a path where your goals stretch you. You're pretty sure you can reach these goals but you're going to have to work hard. The path is going to be dusty and sometimes pretty rocky. There will be some hills to climb.

This is how most people think of goals – Sure, you need to work harder and they make the path before them to just work harder. No doubt the dirt road path is going to yield much more satisfaction and success out of life than the paved road, but still, the dirt road isn't what you were made for. You were meant for something extraordinary, bold and revolutionary. I want you take the next journey…

Level 3 – THE MOUNTAIN PEAK: Imagine standing at the base of a massive mountain and looking at the peak. How amazing would it be to climb to the top? What exhilaration would you have when you finally climb up and look down at the valley floor and see where you were and where you have arrived?

From up on top, you can see the paved road and the dirt road below – you can truly have the satisfaction that you achieved something great in your life. There are no regrets taking the path to the mountain peak. - Only exhilaration, excitement and adventure!

Here's an important thing to understand about the mountain peak path. When you're standing on the valley floor, you aren't sure how to make it to the top. You actually aren't sure IF you're going to make it to the top. But you do understand that there is glory in the attempt. If you don't make it to the peak, wherever you end up is much higher and much more satisfying than anywhere the paved or dirt road could take you.

Level 3 goals should excite you and scare you at the same time. Just like hiking to a tall mountain peak would.

Making this Level 3 mountain goal for your life's path has immense power. You will need to commit and prepare for this journey. It's not going to be easy – nothing glorious and amazing in life is easy. You need to change your mindset, your habits, and how you're doing things right now.

So what do you need to do to make sure you reach the top?

THE TOOLS YOU NEED TO MAKE IT TO THE MOUNTAIN PEAK

Once you've committed to taking the path less traveled – to the mountain peak – you're going to make major preparations and have the right tools and gear to ensure your success.

Climbing a real mountain peak takes an immense amount of preparation, training and making sure your correct gear and tools are brought along. Things like: good boots, good clothes, ropes, backpack, tents, food, water filters, etc. So if you would commit to this journey of making it to the top of the mountain peak, here are some ideas to help you on your way.

1 – Take Responsibility
Like a leaf in the wind getting blown to wherever the wind takes it, most people do not take responsibility for their own lives. So they are pushed and blown away by outside forces – other people, their bosses, their community and a million other circumstances.

This is not the pathway to success. You must take responsibility for your life, for your success and for everything in your life. There's no blame – if you don't reach your goals, guess what, it's your fault. Not your Dad's fault because he was mean to you when you were 6 years old. It's not your boss's fault because he just doesn't get it. It's yours and yours alone.

The moment you take this mantle upon yourself that you truly are the captain of your own ship and that you're going to steer it through and around the rough waters to the place you want to go, you will be empowered to make it to the top.

You'll find the ways and means to make your dreams and goals a reality. You'll study what you need to study, work where and how you need to work to learn and get the experience you need. You'll put in your dues. You have the responsibility – you own it .

2 – Commit to Greatness

Imagine you could take your pick of any prize you wanted from the "Price is Right" game show. You had a range of choices from a $50 cleaning kit to a $50K car. It's easy, right? ….you'd pick the big car.

You have the same type of choice in life – you get to choose anything you want to take out of it. Its sad to see so many choose to take the cleaning kit with them when they could have the car.

If you want to take home the car, you need to commit to greatness. It's going to be hard work and you need to put in some effort. Here are some things you need to do to commit to greatness:

- Read! One of the most vital things you can do for your success.
- Get up early! The old saying is 'the early bird get's the worm'… true then, true now.
- Vehicle University – Make driving time learning time.
- Think! Albert Einstein said that imagination is much more powerful than knowledge
- Act! The number one success secret is massive action.
- Revolutionize! Those who get the most out of life do things in a revolutionary and different way.

Think about ways that you can truly achieve greatness and commit to doing them.

3 – Set Goals – Climb the Mountain Peak

Without a goal, you have no vision of where you want to go and what you want to take out of life. Goals have that amazing power of clarifying your purpose and sharpening what you need to do – to achieve your greatness.

This is what this entire chapter has been about – how to properly set your goals. Don't settle for anything less than reaching the mountain peak and set Level 3 type goals.

If you don't know where you're going, nowhere is where you'll end up. Set your goals and set them high, so you end up having "no regrets."

4 – Plan

"If you fail to plan, you plan to fail."

I love that phrase. Once you have a massive, earth-shattering goal set, you now need to make your plan to reach it. What are you going to do on a DAILY basis to finally reach your goal? My experience has been that you need to plan when, how and what you're going to get done daily.

If it's not planned, it's most likely not going to get done.

It helps to remember this: *All great achievements are completed one small task at a time. You reach the top of a mountain by taking small individual steps.*

Plan these steps, complete them, and soon you'll reach your goal.

5 – Attitude/Mindset

Among the most important things you can do to ensure massive success is to ensure you have a massively successful attitude and mindset. When you keep your outlook positive and your feelings positive, you'll be able to keep going when obstacles and challenges try to sway you off course. You'll be able to perceive the hidden opportunities to seize, that otherwise would be hidden.

Having not just a positive attitude, but also an intensely-focused mindset that no matter what happens or comes your way, 'you will reach your goal' attitude is what is going to propel and sustain you to achieve what you have determined.

I can't state it more simply – if you have the right attitude you will achieve your goals, and if you don't, you won't.

6 – Creativity

One of the most powerful faculties you possess is creativity. I quoted Albert Einstein, considered one of the brightest people to ever live, as saying, "Imagination is more powerful than knowledge." I believe this to be true.

Through creativity, you can find massive breakthroughs in your business and life to get you to your massive goal quicker and faster than you thought possible. Imagine this: instead of walking and climbing the mountain peak, you came up with a way to use a helicopter to fly to the peak in just a few minutes. This is the power of creativity.

Ask yourself: How can I achieve what I want much quicker? Are there more effective ways of completing my tasks? This one is important: Is there a way to do things drastically different in my industry or life that could produce drastically different results?

What you're looking for is a major breakthrough to reach your goals quicker and even dramatically exceed them. You can find these ways through your own creativity.

Here's a major clue: To get drastically different results in your life and business, you must do things in a drastically different way. To quote Mr. Einstein again, "Insanity: doing the same thing over and over again and expecting different results."

SLAY THE WOLF!

Obstacles will no doubt come along your pathway to the top of the mountain. They are to be planned for even though you can't foretell what they'll be, and how difficult they may be to overcome. These major setbacks, challenges, obstacles, etc. will throw most people off their path or make them turn around and go back home. They'll do the same if you don't have the firm commitment you need to achieve your objective and goals….a hardcore, firm commitment.

Fear, disappointment, failures, working harder than expected, and the hundreds of other challenges you will encounter need to be expected and prepared for and dealt with head on, without fear.

What would you do while hiking along the mountain path to the top, walking in the darkness of the thick forest trees when you see, crouched in front of you, a huge, black, ferocious, ravenous wolf. The evil wolf is intent on blocking your path and having you for dinner.

What is your response? Run away screaming? 98% of people will do just that. It's the natural and easiest thing to do. But if you do that, you'll never reach the top of the mountain peak.

What you must do is the hard thing – the bold thing – you must slay the wolf. Take the wolf head on, take it out, and clear it out of the path of your destiny. Slay the wolf.

Any challenges you face on the pathway to your massive goal you must face head on. Then take them out and clear them out of your way. Nothing, and I mean nothing, will stand in your way to reaching your goals.

EXPECT ABUNDANCE

This entire chapter has been about setting the proper expectations for your achievements. They are expectations much higher than you previously had. It's important to understand that your expectations have immense power.

You will get out of yourself and out of your life that which you expect.

Expect:

- To achieve much more than you have currently planned.
- To never give up when challenges come into your path.
- To reach the mountain peaks.

Your potential is unlimited – you can achieve and be anything you set your mind to, and make a firm commitment to make happen. Remember, it's completely up to you what you're going to achieve and what you're going to get out of life. Be among the few that actually make that decision, and when you do, make it a bold and daring choice for your life's destiny.

About Dustin

Dustin Dart is a best selling author, renowned sales and business success trainer and coach to many highly successful business leaders. He is the founder of the Sales Revolution seminars that demonstrates how any business or sales team can easily more than double their sales in less than a year – of which hundreds of companies have been able to do.

During Dustin's highly successful sales career he studied and achieved the prestigious Technical Sales Degree from Weber State University. From this training and other innovations, he proved how to have immense success in the sales field by rising to the top 1% of sales people in the industry, and subsequently helping businesses of all different backgrounds dramatically increase their sales.

To learn more about Dustin Dart and receive free training,
Visit his website: www.DustinDart.com

CHAPTER 21

A CHAMPION MINDSET

BY TAMMI BOOTEN

It all happened so fast. Stopped behind a car waiting for a pedestrian to cross the street, I remember glancing in my rearview mirror and before I could react, in an instant my car was now sandwiched between two vehicles. In that moment when life stood still, trapped in my car, shocked, and paralyzed by feelings of helplessness, I had no idea that what just happened to me was about to become a turning point that forever changed me.

So much more than an accident occurred on that sunny spring day in March; it was a blessing in disguise that has made such a difference in me, my life, and my business. For many months preceding this day, I found myself soul-searching, seeking confirmation for my choices and circumstances. I was emotionally drained and taking life as it was handed to me day-by-day, instead of me taking charge of my life each and every day.

In the process, I found myself drifting through life. I was married to an incredible man, a mother of two amazing children, successful with a beautiful home, but something was still missing. There was a restlessness inside, ignited by exhaustion and feelings of discontentment. Yet, this life was exactly what I said I had wanted for so long. What could I possibly do to enjoy my life so much more?

In time, I realized that much of my negativity stemmed from my own thinking. I slowly discovered that my happiness had less to do with my circumstances and more to do with my thoughts about those circumstances. Recalling the many emotions that stirred inside of me, I vividly remember the circumstances that I reacted to.

This was especially true when my daughter was diagnosed with a learning disability. I was angry and sad; why me? In some way, I was mourning the loss of my perfect child. I only wanted to find a way to fix everything. Searching for answers, I found myself feeling lonely and isolated because others around me didn't understand. I needed to focus on the blessing of this beautiful little girl and the incredible gift she is to me and this world. Instead, I was allowing my negative thoughts to consume me when I was trying so desperately to find solutions to help her with very little guidance. All the while, this little girl was working so hard, never giving up despite her circumstances. What I didn't see is that she wasn't becoming a prisoner to her thoughts about her circumstance, yet I did.

Almost a year to the day before my accident, I decided I would embark upon a new adventure. Determined to help my daughter succeed, I was going to homeschool my kids the following school year. It turns out this big leap of faith was one of the best decisions I could have ever made for my family; however, at the time, I didn't know that. I doubted myself. I was plagued by fear and self-sabotaging thoughts and the negative opinions of others. I was beginning to see how I lost sight of where I was headed and where I wanted to go. The day-to-day static of our busy lives was distorting my vision – a vision to make a difference.

Trying desperately to gain clarity, I was battling pain from injuries and coming to terms that things were what they were. Being a naturally independent person, many days I found myself wrestling with the pain caused by my injuries and resenting my situation. I really tried to put on my happy face and suppress the physical pain and do what had to be done. But as my family can attest, there were many days I felt defeated. Can't is not a word in my vocabulary, it's not indicative of my nature, and yet some days it made for a very irritable wife and mom, as I tried desperately to do it all. I wasn't always so fun to be around. I had always been a giver, never a taker. For the first time ever, I really needed help and I didn't want to ask, nor did I want to receive it. My pride got in the way and at the time, I didn't realize I was blocking my own happiness and success.

Never say things can't get any worse because when you least expect it, life happens. Sounds so cliché, right? Well as it turns out, sometimes it's the very things that get us down that are the things that give us wings to soar. If only I knew that then, I think I would have been better able to handle my circumstances.

Life is like a classroom, we learn lessons every day, we make mistakes, and we are given the gift to grow as a result of them. The idea is to learn from our circumstances and not become a victim to them. I apparently learn lessons the hard way, because once again, life struck and I felt like a victim.

What started as an opportunity to make some shifts in my life and follow my dreams was abruptly interrupted by, yet again, another life challenge. In the midst of what I viewed as life's storm, my husband sustained an injury from riding on a child's toy that put him out of commission for a few months. Talk about your faith being tried as the increased pressures of life were added to our family's needs for survival. Thankful for his recovery, months passed us by. Trying desperately to stay focused on the things we were thankful for was difficult when we were still reminded daily of the hardships we endured. This put a stress on our marriage and we were tested.

I was being worn down, slowly. I thought, "Why me and why now?" At what was almost my breaking point, trying to cement it all back together, working through the pain and sorrow, the negative self-talk, and looking at what was going on around me, my breakthrough came. It was another ordinary day and I was speaking with a client about their family member's battle with cancer; suddenly my mind was flooded with the memories of my mom's battle with lung cancer. I could so vividly recall her strength to fight this horrific disease, and the lowest moments when she was sick, losing her hair, and fighting for the energy to keep going. Each day was a gift and she found the strength to keep going; she never gave up. She still maintained a very successful life and survived her storm. She not only survived, but she thrived.

It was that moment when I suddenly realized that my life could really be so much worse than it was. Who was I to complain? **You see, I realized in that moment that life is all about how you view your circumstances.** I knew I had a choice and I needed to take massive action to make some changes. This breakthrough was like a shot of clarity mixed with inspired action.

Infused by this reality and newfound clarity, I recognized we all have a choice to view our lives and opportunities differently; it dawned on me – that spring day when I was in my accident - I didn't lose anything. I actually received so much more than I lost that day. Nothing replaces the gift of life to enjoy my family while making a difference in the world. I could see the world in a way that those that enjoy super-successful lives do - much like my mother and so many others I began to study. Reading and studying what makes mindset such a powerful and transformational force in lives was nothing short of amazing. As I read, there was an old proverb that kept playing in my head – "As a man thinketh, so is he."

In fact, we create our own paradise or prison by the thoughts we nurture and cultivate each and every day. By discovering how to harness them more positively, we can transform our minds and literally change our lives for the better. Success is dependent upon altering lifelong think-ing patterns, habits, and beliefs. The best part, this concept is not some earth-shattering new idea. The most influential thinkers and philoso-phers throughout our history have spoken of this concept; the Bible and other classic writings regularly affirm it. But those of us deep in the throes of life can lose sight of the power we have to make a change. We begin to believe that our lofty goals and deep ideas have little relevance to our success. We couldn't be more wrong.

This clarity allows me to recognize the same patterns in the people I work with. It's ironic how that works. I can clearly see how they were becom-ing victim to the daily static that permeates our world, too. Sharing that we all hold the key to unlock a successful mindset in our own lives – right within our thoughts – seems almost incomprehensible to some.

The difference between good and great isn't just skill set – it truly is mindset. Just as the difference between a good athlete and a great one is mastering the mental game, so, too, is the case for peak performance in any other area of business or life. By learning the power of mindset and how to shift the way I viewed my circumstances, I started to experience the profound effects of such. You see, I realized that what I had been viewing as a tragedy was really an opportunity – an opportunity for me to play a bigger game.

Are you ready to discover your strength? If so, then you will be playing with a unique class of people I refer to as "conscious achievers." As a conscious achiever, by most people's standards, you're already successful in one or more areas of your life. Yet, any Olympic athlete, Academy Award winning movie star, best-selling author, or Fortune 500 CEO knows success doesn't necessarily equal inner peace. Inner peace, much like success, isn't something you achieve once. It requires a mindset of ongoing attention, inspired action, and an unwavering commitment. It's easier to create momentum when you're fueled by a steady stream of ideas, inspiration and insights. When you know what you need to do, then you can focus your efforts on the ultimate goal – winning at business and life.

KEYS TO MASTER YOUR MINDSET - DISCOVER YOUR STRENGTH!

1. Get Confident
A champion is confident. A confident person can sit with uncertainty. They are fearless. Remove your feelings of inadequacy. Mediocre performers want things to go according to their script. Whether it's a sales call, a board meeting, an interaction, a game, or a test, they get anxious in the face of change and uncertainty. Confident champions know how to deal with the pressures they endure. Know the difference between explicit (external) and implicit (underlying) beliefs that impair your belief in you and your abilities to achieve what it is you want. Likewise, don't allow past or present circumstances to control your thoughts.

2. Get Clear
A champion is clear. A champion can sift through the static that impairs the vision. Think about what it is you want and why. Have you ever tried to accomplish something new to only revert back to old behaviors the second you get anxious? The same applies to training someone else to achieve new goals. A lack of clarity provokes unspoken fear and this angst paralyzes people. A lack of clarity stifles strategic thinking, and it can dumb down both you and your abilities. Write down your vision to reinforce the neurocognitive.

3. Get Focused
A champion is focused. When you are focused you have direction – a goal. You have to know what it is you want to do, why you want to do

it, and focus on your map to get you to where you want to go. It could be to start a new business, winning a game, or to perform a task. Strategic thinking requires the ability to stay focused in the face of uncertainty. Without focus you have no strategy, which results in overusing the word "hope." In trying to accomplish something, the word "hope" is not good. This word is usually the internal dialogue that masks fear and frustration and you lose your focused state (alpha state) of flow which creates optimal results. You have to acquire focus to fade out the distractions that can easily take you off-course to acquiring a win.

4. Take Action

A champion takes action when others don't. But it's the way you take action that counts. Successful people take decisive action. They take advantage of opportunities and act on them. Perfection paralysis will stop you dead in your tracks, so don't overthink things. Develop new habits that support your goals. You have to break the habit of being yourself to achieve a different result. Take action and replace old debilitating routines with a new activity to develop a new habit. Stay inspired – motivate yourself daily to continue making progress.

5. Serve

A champion knows how to give back. Most people approach situations thinking, "I have a need or goal; how might my spouse, boss, parent, co-worker, teammate, coach, or customer help me accomplish it?"

Super-successful people reverse it. They think, "How might I be helpful?" If you're in business, then customers and colleagues can feel the difference. If you're on a team, then your teammates will feel it too. Share your unique skills, talents, and abilities. It doesn't matter what it is you want to do in life, you have to realize that this mental shift in approach is fundamental to why the most successful get such immediate, positive reactions from others.

6. Get Grateful

Champions are grateful for their experiences – good or bad. They take every experience and apply it as an opportunity to learn, to live fully and presently in every moment. I often say, "Grateful attitudes are the seeds that make souls blossom." So often there is a breakdown before the breakthrough. Be thankful for the opportunities that allow you to grow and develop. Remember, it's how you view your circumstances that define you, not your experiences.

7. Get Committed

Champions are committed. They are willing to hang in there and strive to be better despite the chance of failure. Mindset is like motivation, you need to practice it regularly.

8. No Excuses!

Champions don't make excuses. You've heard the saying, ask and you shall receive. Yet, when it shows up – not in a nice gift-wrapped package, of course – but in the form of an opportunity, then don't use self-sabotaging behaviors that prevent you from receiving what it is YOU want and deserve. What are you waiting for? Master your mindset and go after your dreams. Do what it takes to experience the success and fulfillment you want.

Believe YOU can!

About Tammi

Tammi Booten, a recognized certified professional coach, sought-after speaker, and inspirational thought-leader, is best known for her specialization in developing infused mindsets for success. Often referred to as "The Head Coach" by many of her clients, Tammi has studied and developed models that will assist you with your personal, professional, athletic, or academic journey. With her infectious enthusiasm and a passion to help others, Tammi teaches how to take life to the next level.

Tammi possesses a diverse background ranging from organizational leadership, business development, performance coaching, academic coaching, and even a published correspondent writer. Tammi's entrepreneurial spirit has gained her the knowledge and experience to better guide you to conquer the things that are blocking you from achieving your success. Combine this with her inherent love of learning; it's no surprise that Tammi likes to refer to herself as multi-faceted.

Realizing her love to help others discover their strength and achieve success, Tammi recognized that she had been coaching most of her life. She's an expert at inspiring action, finding overlooked opportunities, unlocking new sources of success.

Tammi helps individuals, entrepreneurs, athletes, teams, professional organizations and students build new mental muscle with strategies that will boost mental toughness and improve skills for performance at their highest potential. Tammi's peak performance coaching will bring out the champion in you.

To learn more about Tammi Booten and how she can help you get focused, get clear, and take massive action to exceed the boundaries holding you back, visit: www.TammiBooten.com

CHAPTER 22

MARLENE GRACE'S POWER OF THE INFORMED

BY MARLENE GRACE HARPER

EMPOWERMENT TO CREATE A POSITIVE WAY OF LIFE — WITH SCARLET O'AIRHEAD AND EINSTEIN, THE PUPPET.

Just before my sixth birthday, personal events shaped the future of my World, spinning it 360 degrees. My father, who was a doctor and had heart problems, passed away. When I was born, he and my mother were going to the University of Toronto, so my parents had put off having more children. They were just getting ready to have more babies when he had the fatal heart attack. So, I grew up as an only child and as the center of my mother's life. Her life revolved around my life.

Because of this, I've always had an involvement with life-and-death issues and was also concerned about one-parent families. There weren't many one-parent families when I was growing up, but it's very common now. This is an epidemic and universal problem in our society. Also there are many people, especially baby boomers, who have lost family members, so a large part of what I do is help people cope with the loss of a loved one. I can extend a hand to someone who has said farewell to their spouse and sweetheart.

I have a lot of empathy and insight, because of my personal experiences, so I teach at schools and work with teenagers frequently. Growing up was difficult on several levels. I was pretty small when I went to high school myself; I had actually stopped growing for two years because of the shock of my father's passing. Being the smallest in high school was interesting as I looked like I was still in elementary school.

I found there were many things done to help adjust. The primary force was performing in the theater. My smallness yet maturity in age helped in landing some terrific roles. My stage families became important.

Einstein, the puppet, tells part of my story. He helps get a needed point across, with brilliance. I am a Puppeteer, with over three hundred characters. Known for puppet trees (like a Christmas tree or Hanukkah Bush - only filled with puppets), this arsenal of fun puppets are my assistants for creating action and sometimes release. They help a child express feelings of something not good or harsh on their little life. Why puppets? Children can communicate with a puppet or Teddy Bear and say things or relate more than to an adult, so are more apt to talk to them for healing and interaction. With these assistants, students can speak out their pain and begin to heal.

Puppets are a great therapy. In one program, I had thirty different animal and people puppets we were working with. Before we started, a two year old who was with his family went to the display table and picked out the puppet that looked like a mother. He dragged it around by the tongue. His mother was surprised and then confessed that she had been upset earlier in the day and was yelling. She realized the impact it had on her child and worked to remedy the situation.

We have crafted a new brand of inspiring and uplifting puppets, we call them "Up Pets."

One of the hardest parts of doing what I do is seeing our youth with low self-esteem and little hope for the future. I've seen and worked with a lot of teenagers. I have known of some who have even committed suicide. I've had to be the teacher to tell classmates that one of their friends is no longer with us. That's really tough! I want to do programs that empower young people so they know they are leaders and the hope for the future.

When the going gets tough, we get tougher...what keeps me going is humor. I love the theater and I take laughter's last stand! The most important thing about comedy is timing, and that produces humor. Getting through life with a smile, when things are really tough, and saying, "Well, this is all material for the book!" really helps.

Bullying is a major challenge in our society. Poor self-esteem can lead to Bullying. Often bullies come in many shapes and sizes. We have the abused person who becomes the strike-out bully or one who is jealous of the smarter or richer. We also have the popular romantic, who is a Casanova Bully.

Now, how can a teenager as an innocent bystander to life and a junior high school student avoid being taunted by rough girls sitting on a wall across the street from the school, smoking. Or picture being chased home by the 'wannabe' football guy who isn't talented enough to make the Varsity team, but is tough enough to get a couple of buds to join in while he beats on someone after school.

Becoming a weightlifter is a possibility, or learning how to have big guys as your friends for safety in numbers may or may not do the trick. Yet, can we help these young people make better life decisions and be more informed? You bet. There are benefits of being properly equipped to handle these situations.

I find it rewarding getting people to live and find their potential. I love putting people on pedestals and helping them empower themselves. My program, "UBU Bound Youth Empowerment," means You Be You, and teaches being the best you can be. We do that with theater, writing, art, and schoolwork. There are many opportunities out there. We live in a negative society. We want young people to have realistic goals and still know that the sky's the limit and opportunities are limitless.

The students who really benefit from my You Be You program go on to do a program called "Turn it Around Compliment Bound," where we actually do artwork and writing, and combine the left and right brain. The young people who are struggling really get it, and it gives them a lot of hope. The young people who are gifted, and who get bored in school, love it because it gives them a new creative outlet.

We have a witty put-up formula, called "POPS". It stands for:

P = Put-Ups

O= Overboard which/witch is exaggeration for comic effect

P= Playing with words

S= Suspense, silliness, senses 5, sensational, and surprise

Example: Why Scarlet, you are so sweet, people are happy just to lick your picture.

My mission is: I create. I love to create whatever we create. We create our joy, our happiness, and our ability to cope with whatever's going on. I've worked with teenagers who have had brothers or sisters who have been killed in car accidents, and it's really rewarding to help them get through that.

I have witnessed inspiring transformation or manifestation in my work.

We're working with life and death on many, many levels. The key is that you can live your life to the fullest—that you can be you, be yourself, be who you're meant to be, be empowered—and create the life that you want to create.

Why Scarlet?

She has red hair; a humorous element, plays with words and is always up. She has a sister Amelia Airhead, a pilot who is always getting lost, and a cousin Anita Bathe, who comes in handy with her bar of soap when language needs to be cleaned up.

I play a character named Scarlet O'Airhead, and I go into art classes, English classes, and counseling classes to help students determine their careers, especially with junior high school age. I dress up and say, "Now, your teacher told me when I finish talkin' to y'all that I have to have a really good close, so I bought this dress and I hope y'all like it." I play with turning the words around with funny things like that. I say that it doesn't matter what happened to them, but I have two rules; one is that I don't accept anything crude, rude, or obscene, and the second rule is we have fun. I tell them, "You'll forget a lot of things you did in school, but you'll never forget Miss Scarlet coming to school. If you don't want to stay in the classroom, you can go to another room and do your other schoolwork." I've never had anybody leave.

I do a lot of programs in junior high, because I figure that junior high, the middle school age, is a really forgotten area. There are lots of programs for children, high school, and adults, but not for middle schoolers. In my art class, they come up with things like, "In my hot chocolate, you are the marshmallows," and other really fun metaphors, and they draw the picture of the steaming hot chocolate with the marshmallows popping up. Or, they might say, "In my can of pop, you're the fizz," or "You make my time tick"—fun things like that. We put up compliments and use the humor for put-ups rather than put-downs. I gathered the work from one particular art class and noticed there were over 30 pictures by the same artist. There was no name on most of them, but I realized this project was suddenly therapy. Children who are struggling don't just do one picture; they do many pictures.

When I teach a class, I say, "It doesn't matter what's happened to you. You can get through this. We can put it up." They called Einstein an idiot and he became Man of the Century. So I say, "If anybody ever calls you an idiot, you can say, 'I'm on the path to genius.'"

On one paper, I noticed a girl of 13 had drawn an elegant knight and said, "If I was a knight, you'd be my armor," and some other really beautiful metaphors. I said to the teacher, "I really feel this work is therapy." By the time I returned to teach the next class, this youth was gone. Her mother had died of cancer and her father had committed suicide the Saturday before my class. Social services had taken the girl out of the home because she had to take care of her little brother. I had provided therapy to help her get through that situation. I, of course, had no idea whatever became of her, but I was really grateful I had been there for her that day. I know I've helped other children.

One day, I had a particular English class. Their parents were drug addicts and alcoholics. The teacher said it was her worst class. We started the class and I took them to another planet, where we drank the water, put on our oxygen, did our brain gym, cross crawl, and linked the right and left brain together. I told them that whatever problems they had were left behind on Earth and we were there to create. At the end of the class, the students gathered around me and said they had so much fun.

The teacher said, "I cannot believe this! This is such a tough class. Some of this artwork they did was phenomenal. I want you to do that for all the classes."

As I taught them, whatever happened, we turned around and put things up. That was a pretty profound experience, to realize something so easy. But when you're a teenager, you don't realize how profound an effect something like that can have.

Shortly before my Mother passed away, there was an Indian boy in British Columbia who was around 12 years old.

He jumped off the Pattullo Bridge and my mom said to me, "Your program's not working."

I said, "Mom, my program is working, but it needs to work; it needs to get out there."

At a middle school, one of the boys called a 14-year-old girl a slut, during lunch hour. She then threatened to kill him. Her friends suggested she do what Scarlet had said, and turned it around with clever words. The hostile situation was defused. When I was relating this incident to some seventh graders, the English Teacher said this is what happened to her 14 year-old granddaughter, Robin. They called her a slut on a Friday. After school she went home, thinking life was over and shot herself. Her life was ended. If she had these skills to turn it around, said her grandmother, "Robin would still be with us."

Can we help people make better life decisions? Yes.

I think of my mom's words often, and I know it's really important that we contact teenagers because sometimes they don't have a lot of friends, and if you can be the one person for them, it will make a difference in their lives. That's what it's about—being that one person that can be there to help.

History repeats itself. Now I'm a new widow. So, again, I'm dealing with life and death. My husband, who was only 58 years old, had a heart attack. I'm creating a new program to empower teenagers and young people as well as widows and widowers. I've also started a new website to help widows: www.MarleneGrace.com. We're dealing with things that you might not think of when you lose a spouse. So we're forming a community to support you as you get through this initial shock, because it is a shock to your system!

Baby boomers beware; it's time to manage the inevitable. Do not be blindsided.

Life happens and so does Death…We need to be prepared to deal with this set of challenges and then move on.

Be in charge of events. I am working with a new Widow, Linda. We know because we have been there.

We suggest for you to have an open dialogue with Family and Employees for prospects of "Sudden Death." Brain Storm. Create a game plan and a checklist to check off completed items.

HOW TO BE EMPOWERED AFTER THE LOSS OF A LOVED ONE.

What are the steps necessary to take when your spouse or child is dying or has recently died?

- Be prepared. Have all necessary documentation in order.
- Have a copy of the will. A binder or two is helpful. With any unexpected calamity, documents in the 'Family Binder' can help reunite the family and protect against identity theft.
- Find your A team to support you. It can be family, friends or professionals.
- Keep out-of-state phone numbers to achieve contact with your team.

Step 1.

How many death certificates do I need? At least have 15 – 20, depending on activity level of spouse.

Why? I needed to send five to our employer, to wages, personnel, 401 K retirement, life insurance and medical. One was also required to be sent to his fitness gym to cancel membership.

Taking Charge of Financial areas. Find the professional help needed.

Step 2.
Contact Work or Social Security. Manage your environment.

Step 3.
Dealing with Medical Bills, Hospitals and Doctors.

Have medical information and medical numbers. – Accounts and phone numbers for medical history is imperative.

Remember to take care of yourself. Avoid disease, or dis-ease by managing your environment.

Step 4.
Contacting Banks and other institutions. Have bank account numbers.

Have deeds to house, other properties, and car. Have Life Insurance policies, Birth Certificates, Marriage Licenses, 401 K retirement and Pension plans.

Step 5.
Four months after husband's passing, I received a letter saying, "We feel you have lost the ability to earn money."

Send death certificates to Credit Agencies: Trans Union, Equifax and Experian.

Use last four numbers of the deceased Social Security Number. Write a letter saying mark this account and code it as deceased.

Be sure to request credit reports, for the deceased and yourself.

Step 6.
The grieving cycle is seven areas. It starts with anger and finishes with acceptance.

Step 7.
Reintegration, moving back into Society.

SOCIALIZING

Manage survival.

How to watch out for Romantic Casanovas.

Time for you to move forward. Your loved one would want you to.

With Businesses have an 'Inventory Business Model' = XYZ for better results.

Make sure to take responsible action steps. This is your time now for action.

If you enjoyed these informative tips and would like to learn more, or to write your comments about these tips visit our blog: http://marlenegrace.com.

You can have hope and learn how to "Turn It Around"...

Remember the moment you walk into a room the average IQ shoots way up.

You have the Power "To Turn It Around" and be "Compliment Bound," with whatever life throws your way or direction.

About Marlene

Marlene Grace Harper is known as the Creator of the "Turn It Around" program, which she developed; and "UBU Bound Youth Empowerment" Society. ('UBU' stands for 'You Be Yourself'.)

She is an actress, writer, director and a puppeteer. She has spent a lifetime working in different levels of theater, including writing and directing productions. Locally, she's acted in over 20 shows at the Heritage Theatre. She performed puppetry with Susan Neidert at Fine Arts Center. She's a core actress in the Martin Harris Pageant, and internationally she has performed and toured in British Columbia, Canada.

Marlene has a B.F.A. Degree, major in Theatre and a minor in Communication, from Utah State University (USU), a Master of Arts in Education from George Wythe University, (GWU) and is currently working on her Doctorate in Education and Constitutional Law at GWU.

Her work as a parent of four, with youth, local community and in the arts has been met with much recognition and appreciation. Marlene has received many awards including "Woman of the Year" (American Biographical Institute), an International Peace Prize (United Cultural Convention), and an Aerospace Excellence Award (Civil Air Patrol), just to name a few.

Marlene's youth program with the show, "Turn It Around Compliment Bound" (www. UBUbound.com) is an established business. It helps mentor young people to take whatever has happened to them and learn from these experiences and move forward. She said, "We offer tools to be successful in areas from financial to thinking outside the box. Our main platform is 'UP'." When visiting Hawaii, a government official called her an 'Island Lifter'.

She is a director with "Wind In My Feathers" – an educational project out of New Orleans that works with live raptors.

Her newest project (www.marlenegrace.com) is about empowering people who have lost loved ones, especially a spouse. Marlene says, "Taxes and death are unavoidable, therefore we must be fully prepared when the time comes."

To find out more: www.marlenegrace.com or www.UBUbound.com
801-791-7630

CHAPTER 23

UNLEASH YOUR MAVERICK MOJO AND BE WHO YOU ARE

BY CORINNE RITA

Life is either a daring adventure, or nothing.
~ Helen Keller

When do you feel radiantly alive?

Are you there now?

If you think it's about your business, it is.

And it isn't.

It's about your life.

YOUR BUSINESS REFLECTS WHO YOU ARE <u>BEING</u>

Feeling everything—passion, joy, excitement, uncertainty, doubt, shame, craziness and fear, and being willing to boldly remain myself has brought me an extraordinary life. I've done whatever I made the decision to do. I've reinvented my work across industries and professions. If I told you my story you'd think I made it up. The reality of it is that I did! And I continue to do so. You can too. We create our reality in business and life. Life is a process. Who you were may not be who you are becoming. Your values could shift in importance and call out different strengths. What matters is remaining true to the unique unfolding of your life. Be who you are. Every moment you breathe is your time alive.

If you are not doing what you love you, you have a choice to create what you do love. Your responsibility is to take nothing for granted and to live your gifts. *Why would you ever choose to be less than who you are?*

WHEN DO YOU FEEL RADIANTLY ALIVE?

Call to mind a peak experience in your life. Right now! Feel yourself shiver with anticipation. Let your heart pound with excitement. Make this moment matter. Make it feel like the blazing intensity of fire and the absolute stillness of an icy pond all at once. *Do you have it? Where are you? What are you doing? Are you with anyone? What are you feeling? Are the colors vivid? What can you taste and smell? What's happening for you?*

Be in it. Write it out in detail. Read it. Now close your eyes and be in it. Be in it. Be radiantly alive.

BECOME AWARE

Breathing into that experience, ask: *What shifted? What's different for me? What's significant about reliving who I was at one of the best times of my life? Where am I now? What am I now aware of about myself? What did I rediscover?*

Write it down.

DID YOU DO THE EXERCISE?

Here's my memory. So there I was in Tokyo. Eyes wide open, heart in my throat, jet lagged and confused in a taxi staring up at buildings that made NYC the size of a gecko. Was I really here? And with my Mom? K-san was gesturing to the white-gloved driver to stop at a sushi-ya. The initial shock of being greeted by two men bowing deeply while yelping Miss Corinne through fits of giggles gave way to wonder. We were really in Japan. I'd been invited to do a national speaking tour. My products were sold throughout Japan in multiple channels. Department stores, luxury goods boutiques, garden shops, home furnishings, clothing stores, really every conceivable place I could think of marketing a unique design. I'd no idea what I was going to speak about or how I was advertised until the week before we left. They just wanted me in Japan. Sales skyrocket when a company founder, the literal life and soul of the brand, directly interacts with consumers.

LISTEN FULLY THIS VERY MOMENT

Remember that. Your job is to create a following from the strength of who you are. Our following came naturally from sharing authentically our vision, our story and ultimately ourselves. Although I was "the brand" in Japan, my Mom was integral to my success. Taking my Mom on this adventure was my only stipulation because you only live once.

Never mind that I was terrified of flying, I had to go. When I write terrified, I mean serious panic attacks on the scale of OMG, ...am I dying? ...What is wrong with me? ...I must be insane, help me now, get me out of here terror. I couldn't drive down the highway at one point in my early 20's it was so bad. But that's a different story.

So there we were. The shorter man understood and spoke a little English. The tall man laughed a lot. No English. I spoke passable Japanese. I learned they had no idea who we were. In fact, they were chemical engineers! Their division of the trading company had nothing to do with our products, but as good 'salarymen', their job was to treat us like American Royalty.

ANYTHING IS POSSIBLE

Speaking of icons, did I mention I'd been billed as "an Urban Martha Stewart" throughout Japan? Yes, you read that right. Maybe it was a lost in translation moment. She'd been our customer. But I am not her. I'm me. The tour was advertised and it was up to me with a week's notice to summon my inner Martha. No small feat. Take her qualities and make them Urban, and all about me? Ok. I'm an artist. I can do this! Showcase your American Style Design. Easy. And do demonstrations like Martha with your garden pots and vases. Oh my. Wondering what'd come next, I scrunched over in the tiny round portal bathroom looking out the tiny round window of our skyscraper hotel – feeling like I'd climbed 'through the Looking Glass' and 'on board the Yellow Submarine.'

CONNECT TO THE BEING BEHIND
THE DOING AND HAVING

Can you feel my memory and know who I am through it? We haven't met, but I'll bet you have an idea of what moves me. How about you? What did it feel like for you to be in that place where anything is possible? Your peak experience probably had an element of what felt like magic. Is your heart racing with knowing your own potential again? What did you rediscover about yourself?

PRACTICE SELF – DISCOVERY

In doing this exercise, I re-learned that if I defined myself by potential problems, I'd never have had the courage to throw all that I am into business. I developed what was initially an experiment to see what might be possible into international wholesale, retail and private design divisions. I did not do it alone. My family provided the opportunity with their belief in me. That's why Mom came with me to Japan. I wish my Dad could have been with us. He's always believed in me. I remembered how much I love the people who matter most in my life. I felt again how being in business was about being in the dream of what we could create together.

I re-experienced my audacity and determination. I felt that rush of pushing myself to places far beyond any comfort zone. I rediscovered how I define myself by my strengths. It was ultimately my belief in myself that exploded our work into an international phenomenon. The best way to do anything is to lean fully into the thing that scares you most and embrace it. It's trying to tell you something about who you are. Panic was a sign that I needed to live larger. I felt again how I chose to experience anxiety as excitement. I trust my desires. I got to live again in the magic of seeing a sea of Japanese brides waiting for me to take the stage. Me!

KNOW WHO YOU ARE

Most importantly I recalled what's possible and what it was like to be who I am. I remembered what it felt like living from what I want – my desires, values and purpose.

WHO ARE YOU?

This was an exercise to experience immediate fulfillment. In a few minutes you pulled the self that you were at a time of sheer aliveness from the past into the present.

YOU CREATE IT ALL

The reality is that you make it all up. Every moment of your life you make it all up. You are powerful beyond description.

YOU ARE A LEADER – UNLEASH YOURSELF

Unleashing your maverick mojo is living your strengths and being who you are. When you choose the path of freedom, self-expression and daring to live your passions, you elevate the lives of everyone around you and inspire joy in their journey.

WHAT'S YOUR MOJO?

You can feel it. You can't fake it. Your mojo is magic. It's what makes you authentically you! Fully present in the moment, outrageously joyful, living your truth. Mojo is the essence of who you are. It's your hidden superpower that shines through magnetic self-confidence when you are yourself. And who doesn't want to be a superhero?

YOUR MOJO REVEALS YOUR STRENGTHS

Radiance is mojo. Think of the emotional force of your strengths as synonymous with mojo. Mojo is magnetic attraction. This pulls us toward action that illuminates our values – our core beliefs. When you are radiantly alive, your strengths are pulled through your being into self-expression. Strengths synthesize your unique knowledge (life experience, education and skills) with inherent talent. Understand your strengths by examining moments of fulfillment. Our earlier exercise was really a call to action for your superheroic self to emerge. *Who were you be-ing? What was present?*

CREATE YOUR OWN DEMAND

When I was asked to contribute to this book, I focused on what it means to be a *trendsetter*. Being thought of as a branding authority, design innovator, and motivational expert has really meant seeing the potential before it emerges. It's already there and you've got the ability to call it forth at some level. I think this is about personal leadership. When you're immersed in your creative genius, your awareness shifts and intuition flows. You create your own demand from the power of who you're being.

In my experience, in states of peak awareness or hyperfocus on a person, product, whatever, what I'm really doing is noticing what's already present. I'm paying attention to the hidden gift and unveiling it. With coaching clients it's an experience of absolute recognition – who the person is at a level they've been afraid to go. "Work" is love made visible – through connection. Work becomes play. Make sense? Notice when you're championing a person's strengths, they move toward greatness. You might hear their brand or see their product because of your commitment and belief in what's possible for them. It really feels like magic.

When you do it for yourself, in an instant you become fearless. So, trendsetting is initiating the general direction in which something tends to move. It's being a catalyst, leader and a role model for the movement you generate. Think about that. When you focus on your unique abilities you have the power to create a movement. I did it and I know it to be true.

YOUR STRENGTHS CAN START A MOVEMENT

My original brand pioneered the green movement in home furnishings. I had no idea what we were unleashing. All I knew at the time was that I was taking a stand for my core values. Integrity, freedom, creativity, responsibility, and self-expression are 'being me' at the level of conviction. What I wanted was to leave a lasting impact on the world. My products were symbolic of a deeper psychological drive. I was convinced of it and that passion resonated. Your customers buy that compelling experience symbolized by your offering. I wanted to inspire people to be conscious of their choices in how they live. Your life is a celebration. Choose your environments wisely. Surround yourself with what you love. That drove me to take risks. The higher value was improving the quality of life for everyone I could. Leaping into the unknown was what made me tick because it was for a greater good. Sounds over the top, but when you're in the thrill of your business, it has to be for a greater good. We all want to create significance and have meaning. For me, at the time, it was designing products with a purpose and sharing the story of our vision. Dreaming the story to life, I was living completely in my strengths. The business was effortless and our success was unprecedented.

BECOME UNSTOPPABLE

My mojo is fearless passion. When I'm there, I am unstoppable. I had a vision of where I wanted to be and made the decision to go there. I had absolutely no business education whatsoever. Zero. I'd co-authored a textbook in psychiatric sociology and wanted to be a shrink! That took all of me. I thought I'd change the world by being a pioneer researcher in mental illness. What I realized is that when you fully engaged your strengths, they're powerful wherever you choose to focus. With a roar, I'd felt the calling to push my boundaries in another direction. Had no idea it would be in product creation. It represented a new challenge. Entrepreneurs thrive at the edge. It's that place where you meet resistance and lean into it, knowing you are powerful. I knew when I leapt that I was my own safety net. *Is that where you are now? If not, **leap**.* I'm calling out your inner maverick.

BE UNDENIABLE

As an entrepreneur, the only real security you have is your own ability. You chose to invent, create and assume the risks of business. Consider the commitment. *What does it say about you?* You are a maverick by nature. Mavericks are unabashedly independent in thought and action with the determination to live by their own values. *Is that an accurate description of you? List the values that are present in what you do. Can you?*

BLAZE YOUR BRILLIANCE

Most entrepreneurs are driven by the need for self-actualization. It's who they're being when they're living from their powerful center. It's brilliance in action. The path to finding your essential self differs for everyone. That's what makes your mojo uniquely yours. The path and the process together reveal it. You've got to find it before you unleash it. Your business as the work of your life is the external expression of it. If you've been in business, it might be time to re-evaluate it. You'll know it if you no longer love what you do.

I think of the process of uncovering your values and strengths as blazing your brilliance. When your brilliance is present, it gives your life immediacy and business succeeds with effortless effort. You are the most unique asset in your own business. The best strategy is to develop your own strengths. Plan your business around you. *Is that how you've strategically designed your business?*

FOCUS ON WHAT YOU WANT

Moment by moment, decision by decision, you create it all. You just experienced that reality. You can dramatically change the quality of your life in any given moment by your choices.

WHAT DO YOU WANT?

Let's consider how you made up your business. It's a construct you've created and its reality exists because you designed it. Do you live in the passion of the inventor working on the invention? Or have you become stuck in your own self-created construct? Has your business become a job?

Take the time now and ask:
What was my reason for being in this business? Write it down! Given that answer, now ask: *What was important about that?* Look at both answers and write:

What did having those do for me and am I there now? Is it still important?

KNOW YOUR VALUES

Am I living my values expressed through my strengths? Your values are the fundamental commitments that influence and guide your choices. Can you list them?

I value being.......   *I value being*...........   *I value being*...........

Are they present in what you do? Are they reflected in who you are being?

We led with the exercise in reliving that time when you felt radiantly alive. It's your right to live that way every day in all that you do. I'm your coach right now. What I care about is you. I want you to live a remarkable life and do work that leads to fulfillment. Fulfillment is getting your wants met. Remember, a want is emotional. A need might represent a rational choice. Let your business be driven by what you want. It's the voice of your true self being known. Listen carefully to the answer when you ask yourself what do I want?

YOU ARE A CREATIVE GENIUS

Ask yourself if you've created a position that reflects a comfortable existence. *Is that enough? Do you feel engaged in the creative process?* This is what matters most. What if your return on investment were measured in terms of sheer aliveness? The monetary ROI is linked to your state of fulfillment. Please do not forget that your business exists for creating quality of life. Profits are money functioning as a transformative tool that creates opportunity. Do you have an audacious existence and does your business have meaningful impact? Be honest.

TAKE RESPONSIBILITY

If you are going to do it, why would you do it for less than all that you are? Give yourself fully to your invention. Ask yourself right now, *do I feel fully alive?* Right now does the path you've chosen for your business lead you (and everyone involved) to fulfillment and happiness?

BE TRUTHFUL – BE TRUE TO YOURSELF
IN BUSINESS & IN LIFE

If your answer is **No**, decide to ask yourself **Why not?** and **What if it did?** The first step on your path is refusing to accept anything less than your best life. It may mean leaving your business as you know it completely. It may mean reinventing the work you currently do in service to your greatest vision.

It's like in life when we forget that what we believe is what we create. Our life gets led by early beliefs that haven't been re-examined for their fit with the life where we currently exist. This shows up as dissatisfaction and a feeling that things are not right. Remember that none of the domains of your life are an absolute reality. They are "a" reality with dynamic and changeable characteristics – based on your decisions. So you have the power to build a remarkable business and life. In any moment, you have the option to deconstruct what isn't working and build what you want.

BECOME A MASTER MAPMAKER

Mavericks blaze their own paths. They make the maps that create their life and work. What we've doing is MAP making. Think of the process like the acronym **MAP**. **Meaning, Awareness and Purpose.** Make MAP**S**! **S is for Strengths**. If you've built a business but forgot your own true nature, you no longer have a compass, let alone maps, guiding directed growth. The time is now to wake up. <u>You are not your business. But your business is you.</u> Its success depends on who you are being. Your choices come from that space of aliveness and self-awareness. It's critical for your success to identify and fully live out your best self. The relationship to your work is when you've unleashed your maverick mojo you are being in your creative genius. Anything is possible. It's not about the doing or having – it's the being state. Who you were being in the exercise is always available to you. Has it been hidden? Call it out now.

Your life is a celebration. Know who you are. Be who you are. Love who you are. Be inspired by your actions. Inspire and empower others.

About Corinne

Corinne Rita coaches high octane clients to maximize their time, energy focus, and effectiveness. Working mindfully with meaning, purpose, and clear vision, you can expect to enjoy a fully-engaged life as well as a more profitable and rewarding business. Corinne's direct approach demands the best from entrepreneurs ready to live and lead full out from their strengths and values. Her individual and group programs teach unshakable confidence, physical presence, creative visioning and living in the moment as the keys to success in all areas of life.

Corinne is an experienced entrepreneur in the global market, a Phi Beta Kappa scholar with degrees in Psychology and Japanese, and a professionally-trained leadership and business coach. Corinne has brought over a hundred products and brands to market with worldwide distribution. Her client list has included billion dollar businesses such as Gap Intl, Estee Lauder Companies, and Martha Stewart Living Omnimedia with work featured in hundreds of publications such as the *New York Times, In Style*, etc. She is uniquely qualified in the realities of business leadership, competition, cost pressures and growth, new market expansion, product innovation, and cross-cultural challenges.

Her company, Fierce Focus, specializes in high performance training and results-driven business and personal development. Fierce Focus coaches work with clients to create and maintain the energy and focus necessary to consistently perform at their highest levels. Individuals thrive when they understand and use their strengths. Companies thrive when they embody cultures of personal leadership, self-development and personal power. The Fierce Focus system integrates motivation and performance psychology with cognitive neuroscience and leadership coaching. Corinne and her team provide you with structure and unbiased support in your personal and professional lives to transform stress into strength and frustration into focused action.

Corinne is a best-selling author and motivational speaker teaching that to thrive in life you have to be/come who you are. Authenticity, integrity and self-expression are core values fueling Fierce Focus. She founded the Achiever's Academy life and academic success program at Fierce Focus to benefit gifted individuals and students with attention differences. If you are a business professional with ADD or attention challenges, work with Fierce Focus to learn to effectively use your unique abilities. Business and personal coaches trained by Corinne are required to demonstrate core competencies set by the International Coach Federation. They are qualified to champion the best from people who have ADHD or what she calls the "Trailblazer Trait."

Get your exclusive Fierce Focus Strategic Success Kit and High Velocity Visioning bonus by going to: www.findfiercefocus.com/morebetter. Connect with Corinne Rita at: MoreBetter@findfiercefocus.com or call 610-293-0238.

Work with a Fierce Focus coach at a special rate as our gift for purchasing this book! Put your learning into action today. Go to: www.findfiercefocus.com/morebettercoach. Receive your strategic success session with a Fierce Focus coach by going to: www.findfiercefocus.com/morebettersuccess.

Are you an entrepreneur or business professional with ADHD or attention challenges? Go to: www.findfiercefocus.com/morebetter and learn to effectively use your hyperfocus strength to get what you want out of life. Get FIERCE with your ADD and partner with a Fierce Focus coach at: www.findfiercefocus.com/morebetterADHD.